MARGRIT COATES is the world's leading animal healer and communicator, and the author of several internationally acclaimed books. She was a resident expert in the Animal Planet TV series *Animal Roadshow,* and has appeared on SKY HD1 *Pet Nation,* as well as on numerous other television programmes. In addition to her many media appearances and radio interviews, her work has been featured in countless publications around the world including the *New York Daily News.* Margrit has also been the Pets' Corner columnist for the UK's *Daily Mail* newspaper.

Margrit is highly sought-after worldwide for consultations, lectures and workshops. She has taught at the Open Center, New York and at Southampton University, England, where she has lectured to postgraduate animal behaviour students. Her work is unique because, besides directly communicating with the animals that she is consulted about, she is a powerfully gifted healer so she always connects with them with healing energy as well. It is this fact that gives Margrit's work its incomparable and unrivalled edge.

Margrit is a founding partner in a clinic offering natural therapies for pets and horses. She is passionate about helping people understand animals, how pets communicate with us, and the benefits to them of healing energy. She lives in the New Forest National Park of southern England, where her organic garden is visited by many different bird and animal species.

For more information, please visit:
www.theanimalhealer.com and www.thehorsehealer.com

Praise for Angel Pets:

'Margrit beautifully helps us see who the animals truly are ... not just our brothers and sisters, but as she so poignantly puts it, "angels in disguise". Through her heartfelt stories she guides us to understand the depth of who they are. They are not only our best friends but our best teachers, role models, protectors, and healers. *Angel Pets* is a book you won't be able to put down. You will constantly be reminded that the animals love us unconditionally ... no matter what it takes.'

Carol Gurney, author of *The Language of Animals; 7 Steps to Communicating with Animals* and founder of the Gurney Institute of Animal Communication

'I see the time coming when animal communication and deep reverence for nature will become the cultural norm. It must, or we are all in trouble! Follow the wisdom in *Angel Pets*. Margrit Coates creates a sound path for us back to what we have known in our hearts all along.'

Susan Chernak McElroy, author of
Animals as Teachers and Healers

'Animals are indeed angels or divine beings, sharing our lives and teaching us through example the lessons we have come to earth to learn: unconditional love, patience, humility, gratitude, loyalty, just to name a few. With Margrit Coates's exceptional book, we are brought into the magical world of the human–animal connection and are inspired thereby to become closer to our source, our own Divine Light.'

Marcie Fallek DVM, CVA
www.holisticvet.us

Books by the same author:
Hands-on Healing for Pets
Healing for Horses
Horses Talking
Connecting with Horses

Do you have a story?
You can send your angel pet or horse story to Margrit for her next book: email angelpets@btinternet.com or write to Margrit Coates, PO Box 1826, Salisbury, Wiltshire, UK, SP5 2BH.

ANGEL PETS

Incredible true stories of animal miracles

Margrit Coates

RIDER

LONDON SYDNEY AUCKLAND JOHANNESBURG

3 5 7 9 10 8 6 4

First published in 2010 by Rider, an imprint of Ebury Publishing

Ebury Publishing is a Random House Group company

The Random House Group Limited Reg. No. 954009

Addresses for companies within the Random House Group can be found at
www.rbooks.co.uk

A CIP catalogue record for this book is available from the British Library

The Random House Group Limited supports The Forest Stewardship
Council (FSC), the leading international forest certification organisation.
All our titles that are printed on Greenpeace approved FSC certified paper carry
the FSC logo. Our paper procurement policy can be found at
www.rbooks.co.uk/environment

Mixed Sources
Product group from well-managed
forests and other controlled sources
www.fsc.org Cert no. TT-COC-2139
© 1996 Forest Stewardship Council

Printed and bound in Great Britain by Cox & Wyman, Reading, RG1 8EX

Author photo on back cover by Jon Banfield (www.jonbanfieldphotography.co.uk)
Photographs on page(s) iv by Risë VanFleet (www.playfulpooch.org); xviii by
Beverley Pasque; 15, 44, 82, 118, 152, 168, 190, 214, 254 by Margrit Coates; 20, 219
by Adele Hasley Wells of Guardian Angels Organisation UK; 64, 134, 165, 236, 252
by Judy Wood (www.judywoodartphotography.com); 100 by
www.FreeNaturePhotos.com; 201 by www.FreePhotos.com

ISBN 9781846042577

Copies are available at special rates for bulk orders.
Contact the sales development team on 020 7840 8487 for more information.

To buy books by your favourite authors and register for offers, visit
www.rbooks.co.uk

Please note: the information given in this book is intended as a self-help
guide for you and your pets. It is not to be taken as a replacement or a
substitute for professional veterinary or medical advice. Before trying any
of the techniques in this book, or following the suggestions, a veterinary
surgeon must always be consulted about any concerns whatsoever with a pet
or other animal. Neither the author nor the publisher can be held responsible
for any loss or claim arising out of the use or misuse of the suggestions made
in this book, nor the failure to take professional veterinary or medical advice.

Contents

I dedicate this book to animals everywhere.
I pray that one day you will be treated with the
compassion you deserve. May your messages be heard
by all people so that you know only
love and empathy.

Introduction

If only they could talk

I am sitting with an eagle owl and several TV cameras are pointing at me. The director gives a signal for action to start and I ask the owl what his favourite food is. 'Cat,' he replies and I hope that he is joking. I quickly move on to the next animal.

Surrounding me are several dogs as well as a hamster, corn snake, guinea pig, rabbit and a ferret. Earlier, a large tabby cat had been whisked away to the safety of another area after one of the dogs had started to howl upon spotting it. That seems to have been a good move anyway after the comment made by the owl – the cat's presence could have caused chaos!

I sense that the animals are as excited as their human companions to be here, taking part in my animal communication class which is being filmed for the Animal Planet TV series *Animal Roadshow*. The animals are intrigued, I know, because they are aware that there is a human present who is on their wavelength and who can speak their language – and in doing so give them a voice.

As well as being able to hear what the studio animals are saying, I am able to communicate with all types of animals in any country. Unlike the barriers presented by human speech, this is possible using the universal telepathic language. This is a form of communication that offers information in a variety of ways, including images, words and sensations communicated from an animal to us at a soul level. How this system works, and why it is important for us to recognise, is explained in detail throughout this book.

Later, in the green room, I find myself chatting to a wallaby, several baby badgers, a lizard and a tortoise, and reflecting on the journey that has brought me here, to this time in my life as a world-renowned animal communicator and healer. As I look around me I am immensely grateful for the opportunities that allow me to meet so many different species, bringing me great joy on a daily basis.

It is a continuing source of inspiration and fascination for me that I am able to pick up so much information from beings other than humans. Communicating with humans is also a part of my work, though, for they come along as animals' companions and carers, and it is always equally rewarding to be able to help people to better understand the animals in their life.

Getting the message across

The most frequent comment that people make to me about a much-loved pet is: 'If only they could talk!'

In the course of my work I have often been with a dog or cat, and heard an eloquent, resigned sigh at the same time that the owner is waxing lyrical about the animal's 'problems'. It's my job to pass on messages and information to owners so that things can be resolved – most often emotional, mental or physical issues, and sometimes a combination of all three. Usually people are amazed that their pet has so much to say and will be keen to know more, including how they can hear this for themselves.

'I've tried but I can't hear what my pet is saying' is another comment I often come across, to which I am sometimes tempted to reply: 'If an animal can use the language available to all beings then why should it be so difficult for *you*?'

It puzzles me why humans think that in this respect they are less capable than their pets. We are equals yet completely different from them and, when we know how, we can tune into them on their wavelength. It is a skill that anyone can develop and indeed many ordinary people already possess an evolved sixth sense. This is an instinct that you too might be familiar with – it might have enabled you to sense intuitively when a friend or relative was in need, or when to alert them to danger.

We can take this intuitive sense a step further when we consciously tune into our pets to strengthen the bond between us. Interspecies communication involves exercising our effective, authentic and harmonious human communication skills; it means becoming aware of information on a variety of levels. A great communicator can converse with any species, and our pets are great communicators.

Pets and other animals *can* talk to us and do so all the time, but we often miss or misunderstand what they say. The problem is that humans today are not natural interspecies communicators, though I believe that way back in time our ancestors were more empathic with their surroundings. Animals pick things up from people on a multitude of levels and, on the whole, the human race has lost that skill, having become dependent on, and distracted by, verbal and written language in order to communicate. Animals intuitively convey truths either about themselves, their experiences, or about us. Unlike us, they are not hindered by the limitations of verbal language – which can be manipulated and distorted – but live within the reality of a complex energy system of which we are all a part.

As opposed to my dealings with animals, with whom I can have a direct conversation, it is sometimes a difficult task to communicate with humans and great tact may be needed to help an animal get a point across to them. It's very satisfying, though, being an intermediary in this way, and I have enjoyed meeting many interesting people through my work, who often become good friends.

Each consultation can bring up a mix of emotions, ranging from humour to sadness, but it's always worthwhile to overcome any emotional difficulties and to share those experiences so that pets have their say too. Humans are a part of nature and in order to progress we must do far more than ignore or half-heartedly attempt to communicate with other species within nature as a whole.

There are billions of souls on planet earth and the greater proportion of them are non-human. All creatures have an individual life force – a spark, spirit or essence that is connected to the source of all that there is. I believe that this life force is soul energy and I am firmly of the opinion that all creatures have souls. Although our world is in chaos we are surrounded by angelic presences which are able and willing to bring comfort and meaning to our lives. These angels are pets, horses, birds, wild life – in fact any non-human soul. We can be helped to find meaning to our lives with the guidance of pets and other animals.

Animal communicators can be called many things, including telepathic, pet whisperers or pet psychics. I like to call animal communication having a 'soul conversation' because what we are actually doing is opening our heart and allowing our souls to speak, and listen, to the animal. Soul conversations take place on the healing vibration, which is why I always listen at that deep level, and lay my healing hands onto all the animals that I meet, if possible of course. This is vitally important if we want to make a real difference.

Pets continually speak from their hearts, and the key is to set our own cluttered minds to one side to listen to this information, then to join in a soul conversation with them. When we hear what pets say, as well as understanding how to help with any problems they may have, we can have more fun with them. All of us are looking for less stress in our lives and if our pet relationships are happy then this will help us feel more at ease.

Pets are logical

From its perspective, an animal will communicate something quite logical, but a human will frequently misunderstand what is being said. Animals therefore often regard humans as the dumb species, as humans are frequently so out of tune with what is being conveyed to them by the pets in their lives that perceived problems are perpetuated or escalate out of all proportion. Communication is about a sharing of wisdom, knowledge, information and love. When we reach a pet at a soul level then we really get to know the individual that exists within. This type of connection has crossover benefits for aspects of our everyday lives, as if we become effective interspecies communicators our improved communication skills will help us become more empathic to our friends, family and colleagues.

In our fast-moving world, in which the human race is increasingly out of synch with the environment, taking steps to be in tune with and guided by animals is not just interesting rhetoric. It is, I believe, an essential skill with which to rekindle our gifts and develop personally. Who better to be our teachers than the pets in our lives? Each animal has something to enlighten us about and that is the exciting part of having a genuine and fulfilling rapport with them.

About this book

Animals communicate through a variety of ways, as this book explains. An important aspect to explore is the unseen intuitive ability – or sixth sense – that animals innately possess. Scientific studies have increasingly validated this form of sentience in animals, suggesting that there is a strong telepathic or intuitive aspect to their lives which could be described as extrasensory perception. Unless we tune into this unseen network and become personally involved with it, we will not be fully effective in our relationships with pets.

Unfortunately our world is not compassionate or empathic towards animals, and as a result a great deal of suffering takes place. When we reach animals through our spiritual senses, we also are guided towards recognising them as special beings that we need to coexist with, rather than regarding them as 'only animals' that are beneath us. Actually, humans are animals too!

The act of embracing each species as valid kin, rather than only objectifying them, will enhance our own lives and self-esteem. Listening to our intuition and communicating with pets and other animals is the way forward to truly connecting with them, so that we can enjoy healthy and balanced relationships with all life forms.

There is nothing mysterious about intuitive communication. We all have the potential for it and for those who take the steps to exercise it, picking up intuitive messages becomes a regular occurrence. For me, it is normality and

I am heartened that there is a rapidly expanding interest in it among people who wish to return to natural ways of being. It's important, though, that we feel comfortable about being able to tell others about our animal 'chats' and I will give some helpful tips on how to do this in chapter 10.

Although the majority of clients who contact me have a dog, cat or horse as their companion, I encounter a wide variety of species and problems through my work as an animal communicator and healer. It is always very rewarding and satisfying to be able to help wherever possible. All animals, no matter what the type, are unique, and the art of interspecies communication is to be able to identify the individual and the message that he or she wants to get across. There are of course many challenges to overcome, but mostly my work is great fun, because animals – when they are allowed to express themselves and be true to their nature – show us how to live life to the full.

People are increasingly looking to bridge the divide between our human understanding and ways of communicating, and the animals' intuitive language system. In this book I share insights into the many ways that we can converse with pets and show how this enriches our lives in the process, as well as improves the bond between us and our animal friends. I explain how and why it is possible to be an animal communicator, so that by the time you finish reading you will be able to practise the art of animal communication yourself.

Through stories about my experiences, I deal with the various issues that can arise when humans and animals interact. By illustrating things from a pet's viewpoint I aim to help you reach an improved level of observation and – ultimately – understanding. This will bring an additional dimension to your animal relationships so that you will have insight and answers whenever you need them.

At the heart of my work with animals lies a desire to understand their complexities, and to do whatever is right for them. Because of what I have learnt from animals I also want to bring that awareness to the widest possible audience, and to encourage people's soul conversations with pets.*

Animals have extraordinary communication skills that also lie within us, but which we have mostly forgotten about. Once we recognise this, and begin to share tele-pathic conversations with them, we will find that animals have fascinating stories to tell and loving messages to offer us. Animals have many angel qualities to bring to our lives.

You are the significant human in your pet's life: I hope you will be inspired by *Angel Pets* to communicate with your pet soul-to-soul and that you will be filled with wonder when you hear what he or she says back to you.

Margrit Coates

---

* Some names in the stories have been changed at people's request.

1 My Animals and Other Discoveries

Celebrate every meowing, barking, chirruping, sighing, breathing angel and talk to them heart to heart.

They are everywhere – personalities wrapped in softest fur, characters in amazingly designed feathers or individuals shimmering in luminescent scales. Pets come in many varied guises, but one thing they all have in common is their angel qualities.

This is what I know to be true: humans are not the only beings who feel and think, plan, dream and understand the universe. Animals are capable of all of this and far more, through their superior powers as angel messengers.

My first memory is as a child of just over twelve months old. I am sitting in my high chair when a favourite uncle enters the room and gives me sweets. As I grab a fistful I turn my head to the left to look at a dog sitting underneath a window. My uncle and my mother are talking to me, as is the dog. They are all part of what I accept to be reality. The people are talking with their mouths; the dog is talking to me with its inner voice. But it is all the same to me. The information that comes to me from the dog is not in words – for I am too young to understand much vocabulary anyway – but it is a sense of *knowing*. This is the transmission of knowledge from one soul to another. As young as I am, through the universal telepathic system available to everyone, I acknowledge the dog's communication by accepting it.

I have always understood that animals have souls, which are a component of all living things. I have also always known that animals have angel qualities, and for this reason we can share soul conversations with them. In fact the more we do so, the easier it is for pets to help us and for our bond with them to strengthen.

I grew up in the 1950s on a council estate in Hull, East Yorkshire, where dogs and cats roamed freely. My mother, whose great-grandmother was descended from a royal family, had fled war-torn Europe after the end of the Second World War, a penniless refugee. She married my father, an English soldier, but my childhood was difficult as he left us when I was only ten years old. In those days there was no financial support from the State and my mother had to bring up my sister and me in extreme poverty. There were no relatives to help us out, my mother's having been lost during the horrors of war, and my father's didn't want anything to do with us. I guess that was why I focussed on animals as a child; they are always there for you with their endless love. We had a green budgie called Dickie who used to fly around the house and sit on my shoulder and sing when I played the piano, as well as pet rabbits, mice and dogs.

The only work that my mother could get was as a waitress and barmaid. She relied on tips to buy food at the end of each day, and if she didn't get any we shared the dog's dinner. Free bones from the butcher would be cooked, and we would suck out the marrow before the dog had the remains. For a kid it was a fun thing to do – and it was how our hunter-gatherer ancestors lived alongside the camp dogs.

I first saw our special dog at a friend's house. He was an eight-week-old puppy playing with his littermates. Although he was a mongrel, his markings and looks made us think that he had fox-terrier blood. He made a beeline for me as I knelt beside the tumbling puppies, and that was how he was all his life, friendly and cuddly. Tucking the wriggling little dog inside my jacket, I took him home. My mother was not keen at first because money was in such short supply, but the puppy's ways soon won her over. We called him Patch and he became a cornerstone of our home, the glue that held our small family together through very tough times. His sunny personality made many a grim day bearable. This funny, loving and intelligent dog was our own resident angel.

Psychic topics were often discussed in my childhood home, as my mother came from a long line of natural healers. Years later, if I had a difficult case to deal with, I would ask my mother to think of me. Afterwards, when I went to visit her, my mother would describe to me the colour, size and shape of the animal I had been with and what happened during the session.

'How do you know all that?' I would ask.

Pointing to the floor in front of her, my mother would reply, 'Because you were here. I could see you. We worked together on the animal.'

I thought that sort of relationship was normal.

There isn't a time when I can't remember wanting to lay my hands on the sick and troubled – animal or human – and when I did people would often comment about the heat or tingling coming from my hands. I have always been psychic as well, having had many bizarre experiences over the years involving both spirits and angels. This means that I am hypersensitive to energies, something which it has taken me many years to learn how to deal with.

Society wasn't big on telepathy, healing and those sorts of subjects when I was a kid, and I learned to keep my ways to myself. After leaving school I toyed with the idea of becoming a vet, but instead I indulged my artistic leanings and spent four years at art college, where I qualified in graphic design. Doing creative things is good for our spiritual development because it involves expressing ourselves and exploring what it means to be truly observant; so this was a therapeutic time for me. In order to become a skilled animal communicator, we need to become observant not only on the visual level, but on the level of unseen energy too. Looking only with our eyes, and not using the full range of our senses, can hamper us when it comes to animal communication.

Having left college in Hull and gone to London to work in a big advertising agency, I found myself designing for fashion accounts, and even did some modelling. It was through advertising that I met my first husband, who had a sideline as a bass guitarist in a band. He had done a stint as a backing musician on an early Rolling Stones recording. Coming from a deprived upbringing, I was overawed at this glamorous world, and within six months we were married. Now I know that a superficial lifestyle such as the one I was leading then is disastrous for me. Being in daily contact with animals, as I am now, is as natural to me as breathing. I became disillusioned, so we split five years later, and this very traumatic event marked the beginning of a long period of self-assessment. Although it certainly seemed like it at the time, it was not an ending but the start of an extraordinary journey.

It's easy to miss the obvious. Our planet is populated by a complex mix of living beings, the majority of which are not human. Yet much that goes on around us reflects the pain and unhappiness experienced by people. When we recognise the parallel worlds that exist alongside each other, animal and human, and try to correct the numerous injustices that occur in them by focussing on building a better environment from the inside out, starting with ourselves, then it's surprising how fulfilling our journey through life becomes. One small act can change our viewpoint and teach us to look more acutely at our surroundings. After my divorce I learned to appreciate the small things and the significant details in life, and that included my attitude to animals.

For the following five years I shunned a social life in order to develop my extrasensory abilities. I also studied the paranormal to try to make better sense of the unseen world that was so familiar to me. And I got a cat.

Casey chose to come and live with me in the way that cats often do. Abandoned by his owners when they moved away, the little grey and white eighteen-month-old cat would sit outside my front door and run in when I opened it. I told him that I could not have a cat owing to my long work hours and associated globetrotting, but he told me that it would all work out and not to worry. (I later discovered helpful neighbours who could look after him when I was away.) So Casey moved in and it was the best thing to happen to me in a very long time.

As you might expect, Casey was a psychic cat and we quickly eased into a rich telepathic relationship. We were soul mates, a union which happens through a pet's angel qualities. When I held Casey I would say to him: '*You are me, and I am you.*' We both knew what that meant: we shared the intense magical connection that leads to miracles.

Without Casey to come home to, I don't know how I would have got through the next few years. Socially, it was an empty time during which I threw myself into my work in public relations and, in my private life, into my development as a psychic healer. Over the following years this special cat began to supply answers to mysteries that had intrigued me for a very long time; in fact, those often surreal occurrences could fill the pages of another book.

I also had two rabbits – Flopsy, who was pure white, and Marmalade, who was an orangey colour – and Casey loved them to bits. The three of them would gambol around in my garden, and their antics were highly amusing to watch. Rabbits are easy to house-train and in the evenings they used to come inside to sit with me and Casey, as I read or listened to music; although it was not so relaxing the night that Flopsy chewed through the telephone cable, or when Marmalade nibbled the laces off my new boots.

Then I got a dog. Well, he didn't exactly belong to me, but to a neighbour. He was called Sam and we became so close I realised that he was another soul mate. As with Casey, when I was with Sam it was as if our two consciousnesses blended into one, which is of course what can happen with animals because of their angel energy.

Sam was my confidant, and in my spare time we walked together for hours. He was a big, tough-looking dog, who had been found at Battersea Dogs Home when he was six months old, and although he had a fierce bark, Sam was a gentle angel when he had made friends with you.

On our walks, the ever-patient, soothing Sam got to hear all about my problems, my secrets, and my dreams. There was a stile at the edge of one big field where I would sit down to think. Sam, without being asked, would sit by me, and many times his fur would be wet from my tears as I clung around his neck. I knew that this dog looked deeply into my heart, knowing even more than I could find the words to tell him about how I felt. This meant that Sam understood me better than I did myself.

Sam read not only my mind but also my intention – even when I was not with him. It started like this. My friend telephoned one evening to ask me if I was about to come over to take Sam for a walk. When I asked her how she knew that was what I was going to do, she told me that Sam was sitting by her front door, whimpering and wagging his tail. All of the family members were sitting in front of the TV, so my friend assumed that Sam could only be expecting me.

This became a pattern. Sam would go to the door whenever I thought about taking him out for a walk. He could not see me, hear me or smell me as I lived across the village square, but he always knew I was coming. It wasn't even as if I had a routine, as I worked irregular hours and sometimes stayed away from home. Sam, however, with uncanny accuracy, knew exactly what I was going to do.

Because of these experiences, I started to send Sam messages when I was elsewhere. A sense of peace always followed these acts, and I felt sure that Sam picked up my communications to him. This was confirmed when my friend told me that Sam had started to stare into space sometimes, with a faraway look in his eyes. We compared notes about when Sam would do this, and it matched the times when I specifically spoke to him in my mind. It was comforting for me to call on Sam from anywhere, whenever I needed to.

Then I got involved with horses. I honestly thought that it was completely normal for every horse-person to hear what horses were saying – not by watching the horse's body language or behaviour, but through the voice that stems from deep within the spirit of the horse. Often I would refuse to ride a horse, having heard its plea for help, which led to my becoming accused of being a troublemaker. It shocked me that horses were – and still are for that matter – being ridden in pain, whilst ill, depressed, or otherwise unhappy. The keeping, training and treatment of horses is frequently based on misunderstanding, false information and myth, and for this reason I have written three groundbreaking books to help people better understand the nature of horses and how to communicate with them.

Owing to a new job offer when I was aged forty, I moved to the New Forest area of southern England. By this time Sam was an old dog and it was hard to leave him behind. Of course I missed him terribly and I often sensed him connecting with me as we communicated across the miles. A trip back to see him was planned – but it was not to be, for within a few months of my leaving he was dead. The essence of my special walks and private talks with this devoted dog will always remain within me.

Casey moved home with me but he passed away with kidney failure a few years later, aged sixteen. I was alone again and after a month could no longer stand the silence of an animal-empty house. From a rescue shelter I got two cats, a mother and her three-week-old kitten, that had been found living under a hedge on a busy city road. Before long I had that tell-tale feeling of being with kindred spirits again, and I settled into enjoying conversations with the streetwise female Mitzi, and Floyd, her naïve boy kitten. Observing Mitzi teach Floyd about the world was an outstanding experience, which taught me about the depth of feelings that animals have for each other.

My new job took me around the world as Head of Public Relations for a global company. I never spoke of my secret life as an animal healer and animal communicator, wanting to be taken seriously in the cutthroat world of business. However, one morning during a meeting, I knew that one of my rabbits had passed away. She had gone for surgery to remove a tumour, but now her presence was right there in my office. How can you concentrate when a spirit bunny is sitting on your desk? I couldn't say to my no-nonsense boss, 'Oh, by the way, my rabbit has just come to say goodbye!' Years later, that same boss came to watch me do a public demonstration with horses, and he told me afterwards that he had been riveted by their response, which had left him with much to think about.

My life changed again when I remarried, and yet another change was around the corner when I was made redundant shortly after our wedding. I had become increasingly disillusioned with the back-stabbing corporate world and felt an urge to get back to my spiritual roots, so this was the push that I needed – and I have never looked back. Since then I have become a registered healer and my work has taken me around the world, giving lectures, workshops and consultations, as well as writing several books. My work is my passion.

For many years I have considered animals to belong to 'nations', so in my eyes there is a dog nation, a cat nation, a horse nation and so on. It seemed a good omen, therefore, to be asked to appear in a new TV series for SKY HD1 called *Pet Nation*. First, I did some outdoor filming with a rescued ex-racehorse called Baloo, who was so traumatised by his early life that he became very stressed whenever he was put into a stable. To be honest, I had no idea whether I could help, but afterwards I learned that, amazingly, within forty-eight hours of my being filmed working with Baloo, he had became a much more chilled-out chap. His owner, Samantha, called it a miracle because the horse had displayed stress behaviour in his stable for over ten years.

Later, I was interviewed in the studio about the piece by *Pet Nation* presenters Liza Tarbuck and Huey Morgan. Before I went on air I felt very emotional. Through animals and their response to me, I had arrived at this amazing point in my life. It was humbling. Because of the empathic questions that Liza and Huey asked, I sensed that they were both spiritual people and my lovely time with them was over too quickly.

The cherry on top of the cake came in March 2010, when I was invited to teach at the renowned Open Center in New

York, where I met some of that city's wonderful pets. Where will animals take me to next, I wonder!

One of the great things about my work is that I get to visit an incredible variety of places and have been consulted for some very famous people's pets and horses. I love meeting people from all walks of life, none of whom would have crossed my path had an animal not brought them to me. Because of this, my life is enriched and extremely interesting.

Of course the best bit is meeting the amazing animals themselves. Let me introduce you to Tom, an example of how communicating with an angel pet can be so much fun.

Comedy and secrets with Tom

Tom rarely fails to make me laugh. There are some individuals who are always good-humoured and upbeat, even in the face of terminal illness. They are an inspiration to the rest of us, examples of great emotional courage. I have known quite a few of these special individuals – except that Tom is a dog, not a human.

The first time I met Tom he sauntered into my consulting room with a cursory sniff around, and then his ears shot up as he noticed my two cats strolling past a glass door. Although there is a cat in Tom's own home, he views strange ones as being something to chase, for he is a working Nova Scotia Duck Tolling Retriever who also takes part in agility classes as a hobby. One of my cats paused to gaze in through the window, which infuriated Tom, resulting in much pulling at his lead and licking of lips. The cat stood motionless for a few seconds, then nonchalantly ambled away, tail erect and flicking towards the windowpane in a manner that seemed to be the feline equivalent of a rude gesture.

Tom's owner Debbie settled him down and I guessed that he was going to be chatty. I was told that Tom was actually very sick, terminally ill in fact, and that he had been given only seven to thirteen months to live. I will say right here and now that this is not going to be a sad story, because as I write nearly four years have gone by and Tom continues to act the clown. He has communicated to me that he is aware that something is physically wrong with him but does not feel down in the dumps about his illness. Although he still carries cancerous mast cell tumours, the disease has not developed as fast as the vets predicted, and his owner is convinced that my help plays a major role in that respect. I always joke to my clients that, with me, they get a 'two for the price of one' session, because as well as communicating with their pets I always channel beneficial healing energy to them. It is this that makes a vital difference to a pet at a soul level. Without the deep healing that takes place, communication would be only half of the story.

During that first visit I was told that Tom could take a dislike to people, and give them 'the look'. When they saw that look, it was better not go too near to Tom because he would become aloof and distant. Writing down this comment from his owner, I glanced at Tom to see if he was giving me the evil eye, but there was laughter in his gaze. I was thankful to see it – he liked me.

I quickly found out that Tom loved attention and an audience, which also meant that he loved to talk. He didn't need much encouragement to spill the beans on the things that happened in his everyday life. From the beginning he showed a really strong sense of humour. Through the experience of my work I have learnt that animals come with a myriad of personalities in a similar way to humans, and that, for example, some are complex storytellers and some are humorous.

It's also the way that Tom communicates his stories that makes them so compelling. Dogs, and cats for that matter, can be either the chatty or the silent type; they can be morose or upbeat in the way that they communicate. Being with Tom is always an uplifting experience for me, even when on a couple of occasions he has visited after surgery or other treatment. As soon as I open the door and see Tom's smiley eyes I feel good. He's not big on tail-wagging, giving a token small swing on occasions, but his facial expressions speak volumes.

'How are you today, Mr Tom?' is my usual greeting.

He normally grins in reply and settles down to tell me. Once, when I picked up on his emotional state, it was as though he was chuckling about something sneaky he had done. I asked him what was going on, and I got the distinct impression that he was sniggering like a schoolboy. Describing a dog's inner world in this way may sound a bit far-fetched, and many years ago I too would probably have been sceptical about it. However, now that I have worked worldwide with many thousands of different types of animals, nothing surprises me any more.

Getting the information out of Tom that day as to why he was being so furtive did take a bit of time, though. When Debbie asked me how Tom was feeling I had told her that he had a secret, but that I didn't know what it was because he wasn't divulging any information.

However, being the sort of dog he is, Tom couldn't keep a secret for too long and gradually he showed me an image of him taking something that didn't belong to him when no one was watching. It looked to me like a toy and Tom told me it belonged to one of the other dogs in the household. Tom wanted it for himself, and in a fit of jealousy he had sneaked it away to another room, where he promptly hid it.

'When did this happen, Tom?' I asked.

'Just before we came here, but don't tell anyone!' I could almost see Tom wink at me.

I need to have a moral pact with the animals that I work with. Although many are desperate for me to become their mediator so that they can communicate with their owners, and show signs of great relief when I do so, others sometimes treat me like a confidante and may not want me to pass everything on. Animals should surely be respected for their own need for privacy.

So it was that day with Tom, as I felt that he didn't want me to say what he had done. I just suggested to Debbie that she should watch his behaviour when they returned home. Sure enough, Tom gave the game away. As soon as they walked in the door, instead of following his normal behaviour by going to his bed, he trotted off into the dining room where he poked about in a dark corner. Debbie carefully watched and was surprised when he turned around with one of the other dog's favourite toys in his mouth. It was something that he was not allowed to play with, but no one had seen him take it or hide it. You can't be cross with a character like that; all the same, the toy was returned to the other dog and Tom went to his bed with an embarrassed sigh.

On another occasion, shortly after Christmas, Tom told me that he'd been neglected. I knew that this couldn't be true, because Debbie dotes on her dogs. What was it all about, I asked? I learned that the dogs had lined up for their presents on Christmas Day – as is the custom in Tom's home. Each dog had been given something different, which had been carefully wrapped so that they could go to their favourite places and pull the paper off to get to the new toy. One by one, the other dogs were given their gifts. For some reason, owing to a distraction, there was a delay before Tom got his present. He had stood and waited, convinced that he had been forgotten and was not getting a Christmas present. Apparently, in other years he had been first in line and it concerned him to have to wait now.

As Tom communicated this to me I could sense how sad and outraged he had felt about it all. What really intrigued me was that Tom had experienced such strong emotions about this incident and could also remember what had happened on the other occasions. I found out a bit more that day about just how complex the inner world of an animal is.

Over the time that I have been working with Tom he has become much more laid-back about things – not just events, but his relationships with other animals and people. In a way, I am acting as his therapist. He talks about his life, what has bothered him and how he feels, and I offer healing, which he loves. After each session he acts like he's drunk, seemingly unable to get down from the treatment table and, when he does, staggering around for a few minutes. Everything about Tom is larger than life.

Of all the dogs I have ever come across his stories make me laugh the most. I vividly remember the day that he started to recount what he had been doing since I last saw him. The information came, as always, in a jumble of images, words and sensations. Then I picked up an image of a man's legs with something around his ankles. The perspective was strange to me, until I realised I was seeing the man through Tom's eyes. I could make out brown cord trousers and comfy-looking, well-worn, tan shoes on the feet. I stared at the item around the ankles. It was a pale grey colour and looked like a pair of knickers. Whatever it was, I knew that it gave Tom a feeling of great anticipation. A fun time was going to follow.

There are many times when I am doing my animal communication work when I have to be circumspect about

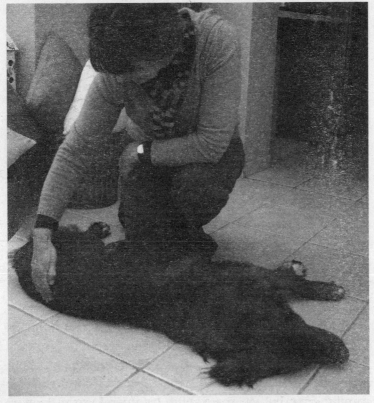

Healing time with Tom

what I am picking up, and this was one of those occasions. When I shift into the dimension of energy information several things can happen. I may pick up feelings from the animal about how it's currently feeling, or it may be a past emotion. I may read the animal's thoughts or I may even be given physical sensations related to its health and wellbeing.

Other ways in which information can come to me include images in my mind's eye, seeing or hearing words, or 'becoming' the animal for a brief period, during which I see through its eyes. This may be in real time or a memory of something that has happened, such as Tom's communication to me that day. On other occasions I pick up information as though I am standing cheek to cheek with the animal, and our eyes are on a level. This means that I am viewing the scene myself as opposed to through the animal's eyes. When seeing the world through the eyes of an animal we have to be careful not to interpret it from a human perspective. We can, of course, switch from our brain's perspective to that of the animal, and to interpret the message correctly we must certainly keep cross-referring to the animal.

I therefore asked Tom what the item on the floor was. He was sitting on my treatment table as I did so, and his reply was to lie down and roll over onto his back. Sometimes communicating with a pet is like working with children in that things can become unpredictable and chaotic.

'You're showing me something around the ankles of your man owner. Do you know what it is, Tom?' I ventured.

Tom had obviously become bored with this topic of conversation and did some more rolling around. By now I had lost the image too and so needed to question Debbie. I described the scene, hoping that Tom had not divulged a family secret, but she roared with laughter. I was picking up an image of Tom's 'raggy', a favourite plaything that was not in fact an item of underwear, although it had looked like one to me. It was a piece of fabric that Tom liked to pull at one end, with growling sound effects, whilst a human partner pulled at the other in an exciting game of tug of war.

By this time Tom had ceased his wriggling and I could hear laughter, something that I often pick up with this dog. He loves a joke, and I am not sure sometimes whether he encourages me to think things in a certain way, just to tease me. Tom has taught me how complicated the personality of a dog can be, and never to take anything for granted in that respect. He has confirmed too that animals can have a strong sense of humour both in their mannerisms and their thought processes. If he were a human I think that Tom could make a good living as a comedian.

Walls speak

The wonderful thing about opening up communication channels with animals is that physical barriers melt away. Developing a healing skill also means that when we come across a pet asking for help, we can do something about it.

A couple of years ago I went on a trip to New Zealand and, after my book launch, I travelled around sightseeing. Arriving at a mountaintop town in the South Island, I checked into a quaint B&B. Immediately, I sensed that the house had a pet, although none came to greet me as I filled in forms and collected the keys. A short while later as I unpacked and inspected creased clothes for something to wear for supper, I heard a voice in my mind: *'Find me, I need healing.'*

On the pretext of searching the public areas for tourist leaflets, I wandered around the corridors, then through the games room and lounge with an ever-persistent *'come to me'* ringing in my mind. There was no sign of an animal's presence, not even a toy or a sleeping place. However, by now I somehow knew that the animal speaking to me was a cat.

Pushing open a door, I paced around the garden, thinking that perhaps the cat was outside. This action resulted in my sensing the cat respond with *'not there, here'*! So I figured that the cat must live in the private quarters of the building, but I still didn't know exactly where. Sending out a thought to the cat that I would do my best to locate it soon, I went back to my room to change for dinner.

Later, after sprucing up, I retraced my steps along the hallway to pick up a list of restaurants from the information table. A warmth radiated through me as I reached the table and, staring at the wall behind the table, I knew that the cat was the other side of it. When I knocked on the nearby door marked *private*, the proprietor appeared. I asked him if he could recommend somewhere in town to eat, craning my neck to look behind him as I did so.

She came forward slowly, the little Siamese cat, a large bleeding wound on the side of her head. Reaching me, she sat by my feet and looked up; it was a huge relief for both of us to come face to face. Quickly explaining my work to the cat's owner, I asked if I could do some hands-on healing. Apparently the cat had been at the vet's that morning to have a large infected ulcer cut out. My aim was to help her emotionally as well as physically for, unlike us, animals cannot have a good sob, yet they suffer the same inner turmoil. The cat remained very still as I worked, the owner having left us to it, and afterwards she purred her thanks. Going off to get my supper, I promised to check on her in the morning.

The next day, the proprietor's wife was beside herself. 'I can't believe it,' she confessed, whilst rustling up breakfast. The wound had dramatically reduced overnight and, incredulous, the woman had taken a photo of it which she had emailed to the vet, explaining the role I had played. As we discussed the power of healing energy and how I had been drawn to finding the distressed animal, the cat herself came to show me her healing face.

'Goodbye, little cat, take care,' I said, as I left to continue my holiday.

Reading hearts

With each year that goes by, I notice a growing shift in awareness as more and more people want to connect with their pets on the deepest level possible. The vast majority of people who bring their animals to me are devoted to them and passionate about their welfare and wellbeing.

If we want to understand the angel qualities of our pets and how to help them to the best of our ability, we first need to become wise to ourselves. We can have hidden agendas as far as other people are concerned, but never when it comes to animals. They do not make judgements based on appearance, age, colour, race or status. They read hearts and minds to suss out our real motives. Animals know the truth about every person, and yet they offer each of us – in equal measure – unconditional love.

However, this does not mean that we can behave in a selfish and thoughtless way towards animals and still expect them to like us, let alone give us their love. We have to earn their respect. It's a question of the more we give, the more we receive. The best that we can do for a pet is to love him or her unconditionally too, for this the sign of true humanity.

All animals can enrich our lives with their many talents and abilities, not least their gift of being able to read our souls. People who say 'it's only an animal' can never have known the pleasure that sharing life with a pet can bring. There is an exquisite joy that comes from being with a pet, because a pet is a divine messenger of miracles that we can become a part of.

Although I had my own first experiences of animal communication as a child, it's never too late for anyone to uncover this ability. Raising the bar on our relationships with pets leads to our discovering their angel qualities, as the next chapter reveals.

Angel pets leave their paw prints in our hearts, light in our minds, and love in our souls.

2   Angels in Disguise

All animals are angels in disguise;
it is up to us to see them that way.

Being with a pet is heaven on earth. We share our lives, homes and sometimes even our beds with these animal angels. Lucky pet lovers can cuddle, pat, stroke and kiss an angel, as well as be licked and kissed by an angel in return. We can be meowed and barked at by angels – and even have one sit on our lap.

There are also beings in touch with the angelic realms who take the shape of wild animals. These animals – birds, squirrels, rabbits, and even foxes, for example – often choose to live close to our homes, their role being to surround us with the beneficial energy of nature. Animals, through their angelic qualities, can bring wonderful gifts to our lives and be incredibly good for us. When we show pets and wild animals our love, we reflect their angel light throughout the universe, like millions of stars.

The purity of animals' souls offers us a perspective that is wholly in touch with nature. In their angel role, pets aim to bring out the best in the human soul too, as well as encouraging us to use our intuitive sense to communicate with them. When I talk about having a soul conversation with an animal what I mean is using our consciousness to communicate with a pet's consciousness. It's easy to do this, simply through a link of love from us to the pet.

The problem with the human race is that we have become detached from the knowledge that all life is connected, and we forget that animals have communication systems more complex than our own. Having become self-appointed 'masters', humans have lost their way. Angels have an all-embracing viewpoint, because they are simultaneously in touch with all that is. Animals are aware of this, and each day they invite us to reconnect with the hub of intuitive and interactive language that lies at the heart of existence. We need to be aware that, just as animals act like angels for us, we in turn are required to act as guardian angels to animals. When we do this, it expands who we are, giving us a higher perspective on how we all need each other.

As you read my stories, covering many varied aspects of animal–human relationships, I invite you to contemplate the angel pets that bless your own life. They may be with you in their physical bodies, or carrying on loving you in spirit form. What angel qualities have *you* sensed in a pet or wild animal?

Intuition is our inner self responding
to angelic guidance.

Miracles

What do I mean when I talk about animal miracles? An animal miracle is:

❣ the way a pet loves you for yourself.
❣ the love we feel for a pet.
❣ why animals want to help you; it may be every day or at a specific time in your life.
❣ how animals know what you are thinking and feeling.
❣ the messages that animals send you.
❣ how, through using your telepathic senses, you can communicate with animals.

🐾 our spiritual affiliation with animals.

🐾 how animals can become our soul mates.

🐾 the healing that animals can give us.

🐾 the fact that, through your hands, you have the ability to channel healing energy to animals.

🐾 the truth that you are an animal's guardian angel.

🐾 the ways that animals act as angels to help each other.

🐾 how pets come back to watch over us from the afterlife.

🐾 that all animals have angel qualities.

A miracle is that every pet is an angel in your life.

The word miracle comes from the Latin word *miraculum*, meaning 'object of wonder'. There are some events that we may marvel at as miraculous but this is because we do not have a complete knowledge or understanding of everything in the universe. St Augustine, a fourth-century philosopher, explains it like this: 'There is no such thing as a miracle which violates natural law. There are only occurrences which violate our limited knowledge of natural law.'

The more that I continue with my work, the more that it is evident to me that animals have a deep understanding of the nature of miracles, and by associating with them we can witness their incredible insight and wisdom.

All pets are miracles of nature
– as we are too.

The devil cat who was really a guardian angel

Animals have their own guardian angels to watch over them, which may sometimes appear in a physical form. This was brought home to me the day that I met a black and white cat at a dog shelter.

The company with whom I have released several music CDs for pets and horses, *New World Music*, regularly raise money for charity and one year it was the turn of a local dog rescue centre to benefit. The record company had donated samples of my CDs to play to the dogs and the centre staff had found that the music helped to calm and relax the animals in their care. A local BBC TV station then got hold of the story and was keen to feature it.

The TV team and I met early one frosty winter morning. As I stepped out of my car I was struck by howling and barking coming from the buildings where the dogs were kept. Some of the dogs were ready for re-homing and members of the public could visit that area of the kennels, hopefully to choose a dog to take home, but too many of the animals were in the rehabilitation or hospital zones.

I was to be filmed treating a cruelty case that day, a honey-coloured greyhound named Freddy. The dog had been rescued from an abusive situation after a tip-off by local residents, who had witnessed him being chased into a river by a group of youths, dragged out and then hit with sticks. An animal welfare inspector had been called, and had taken the bruised and traumatised dog away. Freddy was now of course extremely nervous of people and especially terrified of men.

He was a pitiful sight when he was led into the room where the TV people had set up their equipment. Unfortunately, it was an all-male crew that day, including the presenter, so I immediately went towards Freddy, feeling that he would be better able to trust me as a woman. When I meet a dog or cat for the first time, I indulge in a 'pet handshake', giving them my hand to sniff. After I had done this with Freddy, I knelt down on a mat beside him. He slowly crept towards me, every inch the beaten dog, until he was crouched right next to me. He kept his head lowered, though, his eyes glancing from side to side in case someone made a lunge for him. Reaching out, I touched Freddy's soft fur and felt the trauma in his heart. He was shaking from head to toe.

I was to be filmed giving the healing treatment whilst my special music was playing, and so I began to channel this beneficial energy to him. The TV crew went about their work while I sent messages to Freddy, telling him that we would do him no harm. Gradually, the dog relaxed until he was sitting next to me and his shaking eased. Then there was a golden moment as he curved into me, inviting me to place an arm around him. I felt such overwhelming love for this dog as I held him close. After a while Freddy gazed up at me and I will always cherish the loving look he gave me ... his precious gift to me in exchange for my healing gift to him.

One of the TV crew asked if he could touch Freddy. I explained this to Freddy, and added that he could also trust this man not to hurt him. I sensed that Freddy was at ease with this situation and informed the cameraman that it would be OK to touch him. The man carefully came forward and, bending down, stroked Freddy ... who promptly wagged his tail. We all shed a few tears at the progress he had made.

Of course, after the session had finished there was much discussion about finding Freddy a nice new home and what a sweet companion he would make. I wanted to take him with me but I was told that he would chase cats, and so that was not an option for me as I had three at the time. However, the cameraman who Freddy had wagged at knew a woman who he thought might be interested in taking Freddy, so he went into the office to discuss the adoption process.

After that highly charged emotional experience I needed a bit of a break and some fresh air, so I wandered outside. Needing the loo, I followed some signs until I found what I was looking for. It was a tiny cubicle in a converted stable and, shutting the door, I sat down on the toilet. Suddenly the door sprang open, and needless to say I shrieked, whilst putting my hand out to push the door closed again. It was too late, for the perpetrator was standing at my feet – a small black and white cat with tail erect in a greeting.

She (I intuitively knew that the cat was female) effortlessly sprang up onto the washbasin to one side of me and proceeded to rub her body against my arm, whilst purring loudly. I distinctly heard the little cat speak to me: 'Thank you for helping Freddy today. It meant a lot him to feel such peace.' With this message came the overwhelming impression that the cat was very pleased about Freddy's progress and that it was important for her to tell me so.

I thanked the cat for thanking me and, as I stroked her, she leapt onto my shoulder and settled against my neck, still purring. It was difficult to adjust my clothing with a cat clinging onto me, but she did not seem fazed by it. I thought what a friendly cat she was and how nice that she had come to see me.

Holding the cat I wandered around outside again for a few minutes and information about dogs that we passed in their pens flooded my mind. It was all coming from the little cat: 'That spaniel has a sore back, but no one has noticed; this retriever is pining for a canine friend – the people who brought him here kept their other dog but didn't let on; the brown and white terrier is older than they think he is; that German shepherd barks a lot but is harmless; those two pointers have been together for five years and must not be separated, but there is talk of it; the Great Dane has a tumour ...' On and on she went, filling me in with many details until my senses were reeling. The cat seemed to know everything about the dogs in that place.

As I made my way to the office still carrying the cat, I noticed the staff lined up at the window, staring out with looks of absolute horror on their faces. How strange, I thought.

On reaching the door I heard the cat say to me: 'I don't go where people are; I normally keep away from humans because they are the reason that dogs end up here.' I put the cat down and she looked up at me in a knowing cat way, tail now flicking from side to side in a warning manner, before disappearing into one of the barns.

'*You* were lucky – in fact very lucky indeed,' the manager said to me as I entered the office. She went on to tell me that the cat was feral, hated people (well, the cat had just told me that herself) and viciously attacked any human who went near, let alone picked her up. I explained that the cat had come to find *me*, and had *chosen* to climb onto my shoulder. The staff looked incredulous. They would not have believed what I was saying if they had not seen for themselves this notorious feline happily draped around my shoulders. I too was taken aback, and wondered about the significance of what I had just encountered.

Then it all became clear. The cat was not a devil cat, but an animal angel ... seeing all, knowing all, watching over the dogs. The cat had freedom to roam amongst the dogs, no doubt offering her own healing support and comfort to those poor creatures. She was, in fact, aware of everything that went on and she also heard the dogs' stories, actually having more information about them than the people who worked there did. Even though the cat had not been in the office when I had been helping Freddy, she reached beyond conventional human boundaries of communication, and was therefore in touch with everything occurring in her surroundings. Animals know that there are no real obstacles to reality.

What I loved even more about this event was that the cat had come to find me knowing that I would hear her communication, soul to soul. It had been an extraordinary experience for me. Once again an animal had taught me something; on that occasion, the lesson being that animals have their own angels to help them in time of need. We should never dismiss any animal as being beneath us, or beneath another animal. All animals have a role to play in the grand scheme of things, even if we mere mortals do not understand what it is.

Animals teach us that love has to be unconditional to become magical.

Cracker's miraculous escape

There are many incidents in which people report that an angelic presence has miraculously saved their lives, and I believe that is the explanation for what happened to the dog in this story.

Driving round a corner into a farmyard, I discovered that a bear was on the track in front of me. Well, it looked like a bear but in fact it was the biggest German shepherd dog I have ever seen in my life – and I have seen a great many. As I drove past, the dog's alert, bright brown eyes fixed on mine and I thought, hmm, this could go either way when I get out of my car. The dog might be friendly or it could feel threatened that I am on its territory. By the time I parked, the dog had disappeared from view, so I felt fine about opening the car door and stepping out. Later, the woman whose horse I had come to help mentioned that the big bear-dog was actually very good-natured, so I went to seek him out.

Close up, the dog had the most enormous head, and his snout seemed to go on for ever. From the gentleness in his eyes you could see that there was no malice in him. As I bent down to stroke his wide head and ruffle his soft ears, I was told that his name was Cracker – and what a cracker of a dog he was too.

Alison, the dog's owner, also said that something interesting had happened when Cracker was nine months old. At the time, Alison also had a Labrador called Hamish, and Cracker idolised him, playfully tumbling behind the old dog as he went about his daily explorations. One day, the two dogs went wandering off together as usual, but about an hour later Hamish returned by himself. Naturally Alison was very alarmed, knowing that this meant something had happened to Cracker, for he would never willingly leave Hamish's side. A search party was hastily organised and the area was scoured. Buildings were searched, bushes looked under, long grass inspected, doors knocked on and everyone in the village asked if they had seen Cracker. Being winter, it was of great concern to everyone how long the pup could survive in the icy cold weather.

Hours went by and there was still no sighting of Cracker, but Alison told me that she knew without a doubt that he was not dead. 'I knew he was alive, but I don't know how I did – I just did. I had to keep searching,' she told me.

Cracker was sprawled out next to me during our conversation, his large head resting on a huge paw. Every now and again when either of us said his name, he would laconically raise an eyebrow, acknowledging: 'Yes, that's me.'

Alison recounted how, with a sinking heart, she thought that someone had taken Cracker, even though he had a collar on. He was such a beautiful-looking young dog and perhaps coveted by others. Naturally the police, public authorities and animal shelters were all informed.

Six hours after Cracker had gone missing Alison pulled over in her car to take a phone call whilst searching for her beautiful puppy. 'We've found Cracker, he's alive, but you'll never believe what happened to him,' the voice told her.

Rushing over to the place as directed, Alison found a local man holding a dripping-wet, shivering Cracker. The man had been passing by a house and heard the tiniest, faintest noise. Was that an animal in distress? he wondered. Climbing into the garden, he stopped at the edge of a covered swimming pool. There it was again, now very close, the sound of a dog whimpering. The man lifted the tarpaulin cover of the pool and saw Cracker in the water, paddling at the edge to stop himself from drowning. He had been doing this for all those hours in the freezing water.

The vet who checked Cracker afterwards said that he couldn't believe that the young dog had survived the ordeal. There was no rational explanation for it. Normally a puppy would not be expected to survive in such circumstances for more than about twenty minutes. It would quickly suffer from hypothermia as well as become too weak to swim.

Alison and I discussed why and how Cracker survived. We both agreed that the combined energy of the people looking for him and their intention to find him created an incredible force that reached Cracker and somehow kept him going. The garden where Cracker had been found was one that Alison had walked past many times during her search, calling out his name. That, of course, would have given him a mental and emotional impetus to be reunited with her. The physical challenge, though, was daunting. It should have been impossible for a puppy to keep afloat for all those hours in icy water, yet it happened.

I think that an explanation for this amazing outcome is that Cracker was supported in his struggle by a celestial rescue. How else did Cracker survive, against all the odds? As I had this thought I looked across at Cracker and it was like looking into the eyes of a mystic. What happened that day is something that only Cracker understands. All we know is that he truly is a miracle dog.

Pets have feelings

Animals, like us, have an awareness of who they are – including everything they have experienced. Through verbal and written language, humans try to intellectualise consciousness, whereas animals simply accept it, because they actually understand it better than we do. Animals don't have identity crises; they know exactly what they are about and what their purpose is in the grand scheme of things.

Every time I am with animals my consciousness expands as I aim to reach their level of understanding; I have come to realise that they experience what we do, and in similar ways. Of course, I am not saying that animals have emotions, thoughts and feelings exactly as we humans do. Even no two people are the same. I know how I feel when I am sad or joyous, and what my experience of emotions is like – but does another person feel the same way? We listen to people's descriptions and make assumptions that they feel like us. It is similar to listening to what animals communicate to us. In fact, we can get a better idea of how animals feel, because when we tune into them we may actually sense their emotions for ourselves rather than receive them in the form of a mere description.

Marc Bekoff, Professor Emeritus of biology at the University of Colorado, is an expert in animal behaviour and cognitive ethology (the study of animals' minds) and author of numerous internationally acclaimed books. Marc knows that animals are deeply sensitive, emotional and self-aware. As a young graduate Marc had a turning point one day when he locked eyes with a cat called Speedo, so named because he was a quick learner. Speedo was part of a research programme and to this day Marc can hear the cat saying, 'Why are you doing this to me? Why are you doing this to my friends?' So Marc quietly left the programme and dedicated his life to what he really loves doing – watching animals and helping to keep them alive.

> *Thank goodness for animal lovers everywhere,*
> *because they are human angels.*

Getting into the zone

On the same morning I read in my morning paper that a Hollywood blockbuster, *The Men Who Stare at Goats*, was about to be released, a young mum brought a rescued dog to me – a black and tan coonhound.

For a brief moment, my thoughts stayed with the film, which was based on the US army's use of psychic techniques to kill. Knowing that there is such a thing as telepathic mind power, the US army had authorised Project Jedi, in which negative thoughts were beamed at goats through a mirror fitted with one-way glass. Eventually one of the animals had been killed. Psychic soldiers had originally been asked to practise their techniques on dogs, but they hadn't been happy about trying to kill them – particularly when the animals looked at them pleadingly with their soft brown eyes. This was the blip that had led to the goat experiment, although doesn't it just prove that all animals can read our minds?

During their early research, the military had sought the help of accomplished psychics and one of them, a youthful Uri Geller, was asked to kill a pig using thought alone. Uri, a vegetarian, refused, saying, 'I can't tell you how shocked I was. I love animals. My powers cannot be used to harm.'

I'm with Uri on that one, I thought, as I assessed Snoopy, the coonhound before me. Snoopy pressed his body to the floor, back legs slightly raised whilst his head dropped between his paws. Snoopy had a habit of holding his breath, letting out a gasp and then holding it again. The dog acted like he expected to be brutalised, numerous scars inside his flanks telling a tale that in the past he had been. Saliva dripped constantly from the corners of the dog's mouth. Taking Snoopy anywhere in a car was proving a big problem, because as soon as the car door was opened, he would immediately start to dribble whilst looking fearful. This was not due to motion sickness but suspected to be a stress response due to a traumatic event in the dog's past.

Sue, who brought Snoopy to me, is a veterinary nurse who regularly donates her time to Friends of the Strays of Greece, helping to neuter abandoned cats and dogs in that country. She had come across Snoopy during the course of her charity work, when he had been found wandering on a remote mountainside, scared out of his wits. Fleetingly, I thought once more of the poor goats in the experiment and how my own intention every time I am with an animal is to heal it, so that a damaged angel can recover.

Gently, I cupped my hands around Snoopy's back and sent out the thought: 'Talk to me. Tell me what I need to know, let everything come out. I can deal with it and you will feel a lot better afterwards.' I then stroked Snoopy's head and couldn't stop myself from bending to kiss it.

Snoopy's reply came as an impression of swirling blackness, shouting voices, and a crushing feeling. I realised that Snoopy was recounting the occasion when he had been hooded and bundled into a vehicle, stuffed into a cage with numerous other dogs and then abandoned. No wonder cars had become a demon of torture for Snoopy.

There are times when I say to people, 'Your pet and I are now in the zone' and what I mean by this is that we have connected at the deepest possible level. It is like nothing exists in the whole world except for the two of us. I can hear every thought, feel every emotion, sense the rhythm of each heartbeat and I know that it is reciprocal. It's difficult to describe the intensity of reaching the place where there is no beginning and no end – the heart of the universe.

All I know is that Snoopy benefited from our shared journey to the source of healing that day, and left a much happier dog. I keep tabs on him as he has been placed in a fabulous home not far from where I live, where he is loved to bits. Together with a doggy pal, Snoopy is having the best time of his life.

The help that I offered Snoopy is something that anyone can give. Over the generations humans have abandoned most of the intuitive, telepathic and healing skills that we must once have shared with animals in the days when we had to rely on all of our senses to give us information. We focussed instead on developing language, both verbal and written, and lost the art of reading the universe. Then we got into the habit of denying that our extrasensory abilities even exist.

If we look at what animals are truly capable of, they often demonstrate incredible powers that operate on a level we do not normally reach. Yet deep within us is a place where starlight shines – our soul. We can touch base with it any time we want to, and through doing so our intuition becomes strong again, as does our ability to be wise and sensitive to what pets say.

Our pets have an inner radar that continually updates them with information, not only about what is going on around them, but beyond. Do they know that we are oblivious to most of what they sense naturally, or do they think us the dumb animals? I think it's actually a bit of both.

Animals had emotions first

In my stories I use emotive words linked to the inner world of pets, and so I'll deal now with accusations that this is anthropomorphic – which means giving human qualities to animals.

Let's look at some facts. Non-human animal remains have been found dating back six million years, yet the oldest fossil skeleton of a human ancestor, nicknamed Ardi by scientists, has been dated as being only 4.2 million years old. (Interestingly, other species were found with this fossil, including monkeys, antelope and birds.) It's estimated that humans have populated the earth for between 150,000 to 250,000 years, so from this evidence we can see that animals have been around for an awful lot longer than we have.

Those ancient animals would have been moved by their instincts to find food, by their thinking to plan routes and to make simple tools to catch things to eat, and they would have been affected by emotions when they took care of their young or lost members of a pack or family group. They did not exist in a fog of emotional mediocrity – and nor do animals today, including our pets. When did the human race become so arrogant that it hijacked emotional intelligence as a quality unique to us? Through my work I know that the emotional lives of animals are as complex and integrated in their psyches as our own.

This is my take on things – that humans, when they talk about their emotions, are following in the footsteps of animals because animals had feelings first! So it's OK to use words that sit comfortably with us when we describe how animals think and feel. In fact, it's precisely what animals encourage us to do. For example, it's fine to use words such as happy, sad, ecstatic, depressed, caring, annoyed, confident, or shy when talking about our pets. Actually, the list is endless.

Truth be told, we actually have limited ways to describe animal sentience, as we are restricted by our human language. The term 'sentient' means being self-aware as well as having a knowledge of one's own existence and the plight of others. Anyone who has truly loved a pet will recognise that animals are indeed sensitive in this way.

When we look at an animal, whatever we feel in our heart guides us to the right word to use to describe their situation.

Marc Bekoff sums up the situation in his book *The Emotional Lives of Animals*:

> When we anthropomorphize, we're doing what comes naturally and we shouldn't be punished for it. It's part of who we are. Early in her career, Jane Goodall was criticized for not using scientific methods, for naming chimpanzees rather than assigning each a number, for 'giving' them personalities, and for maintaining they had minds and emotions. We've come a long way since the 1960s in many areas, but unfounded fears over anthropomorphic language lingers on. It's time to put them to rest. For the betterment of animals and for the betterment of science.

A Helping Paw

- You can develop your own sixth sense with the help of a pet. It's important to each of us that other people should want to engage us in conversation. It is the same for pets, who also need us to talk to them – as well as to listen.
- Practise talking aloud to animals, giving them information about what is going on in your life, and how this may affect them. Then instead of using your voice, try doing the same thing using your mind. What do you feel the animal saying to you when you communicate like this?

Sharing feelings: the rabbit who saved a young girl's life

There is an underlying psychic field through which all animals and humans can operate, and we will find it easier to access if we have compassion. It's important to be empathic because that will get us onto an animal's wavelength. We don't have to worry about pets being on our wavelength – they always are!

We can build up a rapport with our pets by spending time together, which can lead to telepathic communication. The size of a loving heart bears no relation to the enormous giving potential of a soul. The following extraordinary account shows us this.

Adele from Guardian Angels Rabbit Sanctuary, whom I met during the filming of *Animal Roadshow*, told me a story about her sister Natalie. The two girls had spent much of their childhood in Gloucestershire, where they grew up surrounded by many lovely rabbits – hence the sisters' life-long love affair with them. Some of the bunnies were kept outside in a big space, and they had litter-trained house rabbits too. Natalie had a particularly special bond with a black and white Dutch breed rabbit called Twinkle. The two of them spent as much time as possible in each other's company, and because Twinkle could roam around wherever she pleased, wherever Natalie went, Twinkle was sure to follow.

One wintry afternoon, when Natalie was five years old and Adele was nine, the sisters were out having fun in their garden. In the middle of a game Natalie disappeared from view and, after investigating amongst the bushes and not finding her, Adele became concerned that her sister might have wandered away. Adele searched high and low in the vicinity surrounding the garden, and even walked to the local canal path where the sisters frequently strolled with their parents. There was no sign of Natalie anywhere.

By now very concerned, Adele rushed home to tell her parents that Natalie was missing and to seek their help. A thorough search of the area was quickly undertaken. Natalie was not found, and the frantic and desperately worried family informed the police of her disappearance, with everyone going into action to help find the little girl. As evening drew in and the light outside began to fade, the girls' distraught father phoned a few locals to help continue searching around the village.

While her parents went out equipped with torches, Adele was left at home with a neighbour who had been enlisted to keep an eye on her. Whilst they waited for news of Natalie, the woman went into the kitchen to make them both some tea. Adele stayed in the conservatory from where the pet bunnies had the freedom to wander in and out of the garden.

After a couple of minutes Adele noticed Twinkle start to behave in a most unusual way. She was in a panicky state, hyperventilating, and she kept lunging at Adele's feet. Twinkle then ran breathlessly round and round in circles before dashing out of the open conservatory door and running up towards the garage, which was about ten metres away from the house and which Adele could see from where she was standing, peering out of the window. On reaching the garage Twinkle 'thumped' by stamping her back feet on the ground. This is an alarm signal that rabbits make, so obviously something was bothering Twinkle.

Twinkle's behaviour then became even more bizarre as she ran back towards the house and sat staring at Adele, who takes up the story ...

'Twinkle actually sat across my feet, which she had never done before,' Adele remembers, 'and, looking up, she made eye contact in such a way that it unnerved me to the core. Twinkle then leapt off my feet, ran more breathless frantic circles around my legs before dashing back to the garage and thumping with all her might. She then again ran back to me. Twinkle's behaviour could not be ignored, she seemed really desperate to tell me something.

'At first I didn't understand what Twinkle wanted me to do, but then I realised that she wanted me to go outside. Once I did this, she was obviously drawing me towards the garage, making circles around my feet to make me step forward, closer and closer to the garage door. In the end I was right next to the door, so I opened it and Twinkle zoomed in at tremendous speed. She went straight up to a large old-fashioned chest freezer stored at the back of the garage which was not working and had been untouched for years.

'Twinkle got to the base of the freezer, looked upwards at the catch and thumped madly. My sixth sense told me to lift open the freezer door, and as I did so I was confronted by my sister who was semi-conscious, blue in the face, and gasping for breath. It was a miracle that Natalie was alive because she had been trapped in there for several hours.'

It was a huge relief for Adele to find her sister, but she was terrified too as Natalie looked so ill. Somehow Adele managed to find the strength to lift Natalie out of the freezer and within a few minutes her little sister's breathing had improved. The incident could so easily have ended in tragedy as the freezer was insulated and well sealed to prevent air entering when shut.

The reunion between Natalie and Twinkle was very emotional. There was lots of hugging and kissing and whispered *thank-yous* into Twinkle's ear, who snuggled up to Natalie now that she was safe. Natalie could feel Twinkle vibrating with pleasure. Thankfully, after a medical check-up and bed rest, Natalie made a full recovery.

When Adele told me this story it made me go all goosepimply; this life-saver who *knew* a child was in danger was a rabbit! The story also made me feel sad, because how many bunnies are recognised as being intelligent or in tune with us? If only more people took the time to develop a close relationship with these animals – think how much better the world could be! I was so intrigued by this story that I wanted to know more.

This is Natalie's version of what happened the day that her pet rabbit saved her life …

'I was frolicking around in the garden with Adele and thought that I would play a joke on her by hiding. I remember climbing onto a chair in the garage and trying with all my might to lift the freezer lid. Leaning over, I somehow got catapulted forward before I had chance to climb in properly. The heavy lid then slammed down on top of me. It was awful because as hard as I tried, I was unable to push the lid open from the inside. I thought that I would soon be rescued, but no one came.

'As you can imagine, I was terrified in the dark, so to comfort me I held the thought of my much-loved Twinkle firmly in my mind. I clung onto to her image; she was after all my very best friend.'

It was a nightmare situation to be in and some time later complete panic set in for Natalie when the air started to run out. The longer that Natalie was trapped the more restricted her breathing became due to the lack of oxygen inside the freezer. She was convinced that she was going to die.

At this point, Natalie told me, she sent out a strong message to Twinkle for help, which she is convinced travelled to her mind to mind, heart to heart, soul to soul. In fact all of those things would occur simultaneously.

Natalie recalls: 'My message was about my feelings of being scared and trapped, that I could not breathe and that I needed Twinkle to comfort me. I definitely felt that I was having a telepathic communication with Twinkle.'

Natalie's account ties in with Twinkle's very strange behaviour at that precise time – firstly the sudden hyper-ventilating as though she could not catch her breath. Then there were Twinkle's desperate attempts to get Adele's attention, finally leading her to her sister. Thank goodness that Adele listened to Twinkle and paid attention to her communication rather than dismissing her as being just a silly rabbit. That would have led to a tragedy, but all was well in the end, and Twinkle's story is a memorial to animal sentience and intelligence.

It is obvious that Natalie was able to transmit – and Twinkle was able to receive – her physical, mental and emotional trauma. It also says to me that during that period Natalie and Twinkle shared one consciousness, blending into each other's soul. Food for thought is the fact that Twinkle was able to plan a course of action that led to Natalie's rescue in the nick of time. That degree of thinking shows without a doubt the high level of empathy and emotional intelligence in such a small creature. This flies in the face of those who say that animals cannot think for themselves or act creatively. As a life-long animal observer I *know* that they can.

Twinkle demonstrated not only her ability to send and receive messages mind to mind, but also her desperate urge to save Natalie – hers was a truly heroic act. Twinkle's behaviour that day was not usual and her change of behaviour was so marked and persistent that Adele could not help but notice that the rabbit was saying something important to her.

Natalie ended her account to me by saying: 'Twinkle saved my life that day, without a doubt. She was a protector and guardian even before this incident, and on many other occasions too. Twinkle was one of my life's soul mates.'

Twinkle lived to the grand old age of thirteen, the bond between her and Natalie deepening further after that terrible experience. They always seemed to know each other's thoughts, and Twinkle would react to Natalie by what can only be described as the two of them sharing a telepathic communication system.

I hope that this incredible story will encourage everyone to look at pet bunnies in a new way – not as a lesser pet but as someone loving who can hear us on the deepest level, and who can help as a guardian angel. It's a sobering thought, which makes it all the more distressing to know that rabbits are used so extensively in laboratory experiments. They are very sensitive and should never be confined as pets to hutches or small runs, as they need a large amount of space in which to exercise properly and be happy. An important factor in this rescue is that if Twinkle had not been free she would not have been as in tune with Natalie as she was, nor been able to lead Adele to her trapped sister.

Natalie and Twinkle loved each other and that created a very strong bond. Love is the most powerful emotion and the bridge that allows communication to travel from one being to another. For our part, loving unconditionally means providing an animal with a natural lifestyle, so that magic is free to embrace us.

Daily, events take place that leave people in a state of questioning wonder. I have long come to the conclusion that a higher power watches over each one of us, human or animal. With this guidance and a pet sharing our life, we are never alone.

Angel pets know what we are thinking
before it becomes a thought bubble
in our own mind.

3 Healing Friends

*Pets say: 'Take good care of yourself.
Listen to me and I'll remind you how.'*

As angel ambassadors, pets play a big role in our lives and the bond between us goes beyond their entertaining us or simply providing companionship. Pets are our healers, and can even continue with this work from beyond the grave – but more about that later. An important lesson that pets teach us is to love without judgement or discrimination, for that is how angels heal. They also help us to understand how to succeed by loving what we do and believing in ourselves.

Deep within the human subconscious lies a longing for perfection. Pets are not fooled by appearances because we become transparent to them. Their view of themselves and the world is not distorted by illusions of perfection or the desire for superficial things, both of which cause humans to feel unfulfilled. Nowadays we humans tend to judge everything by its appearance, but animals have more sense than to do this. I have never yet chatted with a pet that mentioned it would like a person better if they changed their outfit, their hairstyle or had cosmetic surgery. They like us just as we are. Our pets are open-minded characters and do not make statements such as, 'You are a winner or you are a loser.' Each one of us is a potential friend as far as a pet is concerned, but it is up to us to prove our worth.

I believe animals often choose to be with us either knowing that they can help us, or because they are interested enough to have a go at sorting us out. That is why so many clients say such things to me as, 'This puppy chose me,' or, 'This cat asked me to take her home from the shelter.' They talk, we listen (even if at the time we do not realise it), and something very special develops. It's unfortunate when people do not realise that so much is on offer, or that human and animal can share in a healing process.

So what do pets get out of being with us? It seems that pets want to be with us for quite complex reasons, taking on roles that are often overlooked. Pets can mirror our internal world or our behaviour. They can make decisions that will change and enrich our lives, often seeming to have an urgent need to do so. Through our pets, we can make discoveries about ourselves and – even if we do not realise it – we are all seeking knowledge at soul level. Petting a cat, walking a dog, cuddling a bunny, stroking a horse or watching wildlife – all this takes us out of ourselves and into the playground of angels.

Humans on the whole are sociable beings, which is one of the reasons why we have traditionally sought the company of animals. On a subconscious level we have brought animals into our mythology in every culture, and our connection to them appears to be essential to life. Also, because DNA between all life forms is so consistent, it is fairly simply to link it all together. All mammals have genetic similarities. For example, we humans share over ninety per cent of our genes with mice, and ninety-nine per cent with chimpanzees. We even share half of our genes with bananas! These similarities suggest that there is a common ancestry which appears to be shared by all life on our planet.

There is no getting away from it – we need to be with pets. My cats and the sheltie dogs that I look after always greet me with bubbling enthusiasm; the cares of the world fall away as we embrace each other. When I am walking the dogs, we become a team, exploring pathways, seeking harmony, and sharing the pleasure of the moment. There's no other feeling like it.

Good for us

The known health benefits of living with a pet include relief from stress or loneliness due to their companion-ship, reduced blood pressure and cholesterol levels, and a smaller risk of heart attack. Stroking a pet is calming, and schools with a pet corner report an improvement in pupil behaviour. Other studies suggest that kids growing up in a pet-friendly home will have less risk of developing allergies and asthma. A report published in 2007 by the Mental Health Foundation and Age Concern showed that pets are one of the six major factors in maintaining the health of older people. Having a dog also increases our opportunities for outdoor activities and socialisation no matter what age we are.

Pets can have the patience of a saint but that is often tested by the way we behave and our busy lifestyles. Animals recognise that we are on a learning curve and will make mistakes – and I am personally indebted to several pets who have not given up on me for being stupid and thoughtless from time to time. A pet's patience, generosity and capacity for forgiveness is humbling. I strive to become more like them.

I have felt, for many years, that the animals wanted me to write this book. When the commission came, new doors opened as pets with fascinating stories entered my life. It seemed to me that somehow the animals knew there was an opportunity to pass on their messages and to get into print.

To help gather my thoughts, I sent out a questionnaire to people around the world. One of the questions that I asked was: 'What would your life be like, without pets to share it with?'

When the replies came back I could feel the energy of outrage, and sadness, that such a state could ever be contemplated. Everyone felt the same way and comments included:

'I can't imagine it and I don't want to'; *'meaningless'*; *'every day a waste'*; *'destitute'*; *'sad and overwhelming'*; *'empty'*; *'no purpose'*; *'dreadful'*; *'I think a life without pets would be like a life without relationships or loved ones'*; *'it would be a half life – incomplete'*; *'lonely'*; *'my heart would break without a huggy angel by my side'* ... *'would miss the love'*.

No one said that their life would be easier without pets to look after, or that they could find something else to fill their time. These comments illustrate the deep need, encoded within us, that makes humans seek relationships with animals. Once we realise this, it can make us see them in a different way, and even increase our respect for their spiritual generosity and amazing powers.

Another question on my list was about what messages animals give us, and a common answer was 'messages of love'. As I found out myself, a pet can love us to the point of making drastic sacrifices.

Healed by a cat

I have found that two things are constant and true for all beings – firstly that life has a way of suddenly changing, and secondly that everything will come to an end. We can go along on the crest of a wave, thinking that things couldn't be better, when in a flash it all changes, and a high mood plummets to the depths of despair. I have had plenty of those times in my life and often the friend who has helped me through has been a pet.

Several years ago, on a hot summer's day just after my birthday, I popped into my local market town to do some shopping. After checking out the local boutique and trying on a few things in a sale, I made my way to a mobile unit for a routine mammogram. The nurse and I got chatting and she was very interested in my work, so she took a leaflet and promised to get in touch about her epileptic dog, hoping that I could help him.

A few days later I had a recall. Apparently my X-ray needed to be done again, so this time I went to the city hospital and also had a consultation with a doctor. The conversation during which I was told that I had breast cancer still seems surreal to this day. Over the next few weeks I went through all the emotions that other women in my position go through, ranging from terrible fear to huge outbursts of anger.

Having surgery to remove the suspect area was the first step of the suggested treatment protocol. A short while later I was back at the hospital again, and now the next steps were spelled out to me. A mastectomy, chemotherapy, radiotherapy and medication were all recommended – but I needed time to think and went home in a daze. I was engulfed in a black hole and no matter which way I turned I could not see my way clearly to making any decisions. I also felt a huge failure as a healer; after all, if my body had succumbed to cancer then, I believed, I was not doing my work properly.

I dealt with the healer-failure bit first by talking to several esteemed people, who all pointed out that we live in a toxic world in which we're bombarded by things that are harmful. Afterwards I threw away everything that contained chemicals and other pollutant ingredients, and spent a fortune in health shops, restocking my shelves with natural products. I vowed to only eat organic where possible and to have more regular holistic therapies for myself. For days I was in turmoil, reaching a level of despair that left me bereft.

I would frequently hug my gracious fourteen-year-old cat Mitzi, for her gentleness gave me much solace. 'What shall I do? Please help me to make a decision,' I would sob into her black and white fur.

One night I fell asleep with Mitzi lying inside my arm. When I awoke as dawn was breaking, she was still fast asleep but as I moved she made a small meow sound. In that split second she spoke to me. It was not with words but in the rapid transmitting of essential knowledge that I am used to receiving as an animal communicator. At the time I was half awake and therefore not compos mentis enough to be able to analyse what the information was. It seemed, though, that deep down – at soul level – I knew something which would unfold later. This was coupled with feeling a lightness go through my whole body, like a weight had been lifted from me. Drifting into sleep once more, I woke in the full light of day, the room warmed by sunshine. Mitzi had gone downstairs and I knew what I was going to do about my cancer.

When I told the doctors that I was not going to have any more treatment, because my intuition told me that was the right thing to do, they were of course very concerned. Several counselling interviews followed until an oncologist said that he would support my decision and I could be regularly monitored instead. It was a hard call to make, but I felt strongly that it was the right thing for me at that time, although I admit that I was very on edge about it and questioned whether I was making the worst decision of my life.

Three weeks later, upon picking Mitzi up I felt something under the skin on her chest. My veterinary surgeon examined the tiny lump and said that he thought it was a cyst but that he would operate to be sure. It took a few days for the biopsy report to come back and the news was terrible. Mitzi had a very aggressive form of mammary cancer, rare in cats, and the report said that she was terminally ill. It was a type of cancer that spread rapidly and urgent surgery was needed which, although it could not cure her, might give her perhaps another year of life. The surgery would mean stripping flesh and muscles from the chest wall and several weeks of intensive nursing. Again I went into shock, but told the vet that I needed to think about it and took Mitzi back home to mull over a decision.

I knew what Mitzi had done for me: she had taken the energy of my cancer away. We discussed it later, she and I, as we indulged in a lengthy and emotional soul-to-soul conversation. The healing that pets offer us, and the help that they give, never fails to amaze me. I contemplated the situation and knew that it was no coincidence we both had the same condition. It was a clue that I had an angel with me.

As with humans, some pets are precise and able communicators whereas others are less able to say what they mean. Mitzi made it easy for me to understand her. I was of course stunned that my cat had seemingly absorbed cancer from me, and I worried that it had not been her choice but that, living in close proximity to me, she had been so affected by my negative energy that it had made her very ill too. Pets are influenced by our energy states and I see plenty of those cases. Mitzi reassured me, though, that it had been of her choosing, because through the universal connection she somehow understood that she could do this for me and give me more time on earth to follow my destiny.

This was another huge lesson for me – that a pet could love you so much that he or she would take away your illness. Now, because of me, my beautiful cat was gravely ill. This may be a difficult concept for some people to take on board, but in the course of my work I have come across other situations similar to mine.

During the following week, I would often sit and talk to Mitzi, pondering over whether or not to take her back for drastic surgery. As much as I asked Mitzi to guide me on that score, no sign appeared with any clarity. I also called a veterinary friend, who is a cancer expert, and discussed the biopsy report with her. Mitzi was not suffering with any disease symptoms so finally I decided that if her time here was so short, she should have the best quality of life rather than be subjected to stressful invasive treatment. Even going for a check-up traumatised her.

I looked at Mitzi snoozing in her favourite place and said aloud to her: 'OK, I've decided: I'm not putting you through all that stuff. I will care for you until you have to leave this life.'

Suddenly Mitzi looked up at me and made her special meow sound. Simultaneously it came to me that she agreed it was the correct decision, and that she was complicit in it. I stroked her and let her know that I had heard what she had to say, that I knew now without a doubt that this was what *she* wanted. My vet supported me, agreeing that due to her age and poor prognosis it would be best to leave things be. He told me to come back every two weeks for check-ups and when the time came he would put her to sleep.

On the way home I heard my angel Mitzi speak to me from her travelling basket: 'I will be OK, you know – and so will you.'

I dearly hoped this would come to pass, for it was ironic that an identical situation had occurred for my cat and myself. We both had mammary cancer and after lumpectomies neither of us was going to have conventional treatment. Every type of alternative treatment that I embarked on, Mitzi had too – including homeopathy, herbal medicine, acupuncture, flower essences, as well as healing treatments from me. That was the least I could do for her in return for her courage and love.

I went to the hospital for check-ups and Mitzi went to the veterinary clinic for hers. She was active, eating well and enjoying life so the vet would tell me to come back again another time for a review. In tandem with my scans coming back clear, Mitzi's lump did not return. The months rolled by until eventually the vet told me not to bother coming back unless Mitzi showed signs of being unwell.

Those months became years and still there was no sign of cancer in either Mitzi or myself. However, when Mitzi turned eighteen dementia started to set in and one autumn day I found her staggering around in a distraught condition. I had promised her that when she began to struggle with her health for whatever reason, I would help her to be free from suffering. So it was that my dearest Mitzi was put to sleep and went to heaven, her physical body buried in my garden with daffodils planted on her grave.

Mitzi was a one-in-a-million pet for the help that she gave me, and her unconditional love. I am eternally indebted to her. To this day I find it difficult to take on board Mitzi's spiritual generosity. I feel that in many ways she is a far more worthy and powerful entity than I am and the mystery of how and why will not be revealed until the day that I join her spirit for the next adventure. Most of all, I hope one day to be as expert a healer as she was.

Our influence

When I spoke to Fiona, my acupuncture vet, about what Mitzi had done for me, she confirmed that in her practice she often sees pets whose condition matches that of their owners. In fact when Fiona makes a diagnosis – for example of heart disease, arthritis or diabetes – she wonders whether she will hear the owner say, 'Oh, I suffer with that too.'

As Fiona was saying this to me I looked down at Lilly, one of my cats who was receiving acupuncture from her. 'You know what, Fiona – you're sticking needles into Lilly's sore right shoulder ...'

Fiona finished my sentence: '... and you have a sore right shoulder too, right?'

Indeed I did, *and* I was having a course of acupuncture treatment myself. Sometimes the blindingly obvious is missed even when you do this sort of thing for a living. My shoulder was initially injured many years ago, when I had been pulling myself up into a horse carriage and fallen backwards as I did so. Recently, due to excessive time spent on the computer and ageing joints, I had been suffering from some pain. Lilly, it seemed, was mimicking me, loudly saying: 'For goodness' sake, watch your health!'

Fiona also said that in her experience, pets frequently mirror their owner's personalities – she often come across a nervous pet with a nervous owner or a hyperactive pet with a stressed-out owner, for example – and she had noticed that calm people influenced their pets to be laid-back. I strive very hard to fit into that category.

Bruno the defender

Some pets, like Mitzi, protect us from being harmed by ill health, whereas others do their best to protect us from physical harm from others.

My sister-in-law Val used to have a fabulous dog called Bruno, who was an Alsatian collie cross. When out on walks, Bruno would show his herding skills by running in a perpetual circle, from the person at the front of a group to the back marker. No matter how strung-out the group became, Bruno liked to check that his pack were safe.

Bruno was a great guard dog but could also be very gentle. When the family acquired a kitten he was very relaxed when the newcomer clambered into his bed, and they would often sleep curled up together. One evening whilst watching TV, Val heard a yelping noise coming from the dog bed and, looking round, saw the reason. The kitten was chewing Bruno's bottom lip whilst hanging onto his face with her sharp claws. Bruno could have demolished the tiny kitten in an instant but chose instead to tolerate its baby antics.

From an early age it was obvious that Bruno had a phenomenal memory as regards people. At the time I lived quite a way from Val and Bruno was around two years old before I first met him. When I unlatched the gate to walk up to the house all hell was let loose. A frenzy of barking and snarling could be heard coming from within and I saw a big dog leaping up at the window, smashing at it with his paws. Bruno took his security duties very seriously.

When Bruno's family said to him, 'This person is a friend, it's OK,' he knew what that meant. Instantly he would settle down, like air seeping from a balloon. He would then sniff you to place your identity in his memory bank for future reference. It was over a year before I visited again and on my approaching the house the frenzied barking started up. I called out, 'Bruno, it's me – how are you?' The barking stopped. As Val opened the door Bruno was standing there, tail wagging, head cocked to one side, eyes looking at me softly.

'He remembers you. He only has to meet someone once and it's in his head for always,' Val said, as Bruno came over and danced around me in a doggy greeting.

Bruno was also a dog who was acutely aware of what people were thinking and feeling. Everyone who was his friend came under his umbrella of protection, particularly family members. One day Val set off to walk into the town centre, taking Bruno along for some exercise. It was a bright dry day and the pair were strolling along quite happily, Val thinking about her shopping and Bruno investigating everything that his nose could reach. They turned into a narrow alleyway and were halfway along it when a man entered and came towards them.

Val recognised him. He was an unpleasant, infamous local character, renowned for his violent behaviour and drunkenness. 'I immediately felt frightened,' Val told me. In that instant Bruno's demeanour changed. From trotting along in a relaxed manner, he raised himself up on his paws so that he was walking in a slow, measured way. His ears also flattened and his upper lip curled back. It was the typical stance adopted when a dog is poised to spring into action. Bruno did not mirror Val's energy by becoming fearful himself, as some dogs can do. Instead, he was ready to face the threat, saying to Val, 'I sense that you are worried about this person. Leave it to me to guard you. I'm a force to be reckoned with if that man starts any nonsense.'

'There was no doubt in my mind that Bruno would come

to my defence that day,' continued Val. 'It was amazing that as soon as I thought *"help!"* Bruno responded in a way that showed me he was going to do his best to assist me if necessary. It was very reassuring.'

With Bruno between her and the obnoxious man, Val carried on walking and safely left the alleyway. As soon as Val entered the shopping street Bruno chilled out and became his normal self once again. He was truly the best doggy friend Val could ever have wished for and he is still talked about with reverence.

Baby angels

Pets often show a protective instinct towards babies and children, using their sixth sense to know that the little one needs their care.

For a couple of hours each week, Shirley had to leave her six-week-old baby with a friend. Shirley mentioned to the friend her concerns that something was not quite right with her baby, sensed through a mother's intuition. Her friend then explained that whenever the baby lay on her sofa, her dog and cat would both enter the room. The dog would lie across the front of the sofa, in such a way that the baby could not roll off it, and the cat would sit on the sofa arm. The baby would go to sleep and neither pet would move an inch until the friend returned. She was a spiritually-minded person and realised that her pets were taking care of Shirley's baby, so thankfully she did not move them away.

A few months later the baby was tragically diagnosed with severe disabilities and blindness. The dog and the cat had both known that something was wrong with this child, so whenever she visited they had stayed close to her, offering her angel protection. There is no doubt in my mind that having two angels by her side would have been very soothing to the baby.

Coco the astrologer's cat

My friend Debbie Frank, astrologer to superstars including the late Princess Diana, is a big animal lover who told me about the caring relationship between her cat and her young daughter.

Debbie had first contacted me when I was writing the 'Pets' Corner' column for the *Daily Mail* newspaper. Shortly afterwards I met her chocolate Labrador puppy Tallulah, who entered her life when her beloved dog Oliver passed away. Debbie told me that she missed his vibrancy and his love, and that it was going to take a very special newcomer indeed to mend the hole left in her heart. Tallulah is that esteemed dog.

Three years after Tallulah entered Debbie's life, there was yet another new addition to the household: a Burmese cat who arrived on the night of an eclipse – an auspicious time for an angel to enter anyone's life. An eclipse happens during a full moon and during this phase the moon can take on a range of beautiful colours, ranging from red to orange to yellow.

'I heard her meow and let her in through the window,' Debbie told me, 'and she slept spine to spine with me in bed. It was most extraordinary. Although I traced her owners, who actually lived quite a distance away, the cat – who I learned was called Coco – would come back to us, crossing a busy main road to do so.'

Just how determined Coco was to live with Debbie soon became apparent. After Debbie had once again returned the cat to her previous home and she had been back there for a few weeks, Debbie and her family decided to go and look at some Burmese kittens. Debbie explains:

'As we turned into the drive there she was waiting for us on our doorstep as if to say, "*I am your cat, don't look at any others.*" Coco seems a very ancient soul – I call her my temple cat. I love it that she was so determined to come and live with us. Coco meows very loudly and directly and is able to communicate exactly what she wants, and won't take no for an answer.'

I knew that Debbie had adopted a child called Lulu from China and she told me that Coco is especially connected to her: 'Lulu had terrible problems sleeping for a while,' said Debbie. 'Every night Coco would come onto Lulu's bed as I settled her, and the cat would put a paw across Lulu's body and purr her a lullaby. She has such a motherly presence. Coco is inseparable from my daughter and allows herself to be picked up awkwardly, even in the most uncomfortable positions. Coco never moves, wriggles or claws at Lulu – she is totally connected to her.'

I asked Debbie how her dog Tallulah took to Lulu and then Coco entering the household. Debbie told me that she is a gorgeous generous dog, adding, 'Tallulah's love is so tangible and she's such a kind dog, gracefully allowing first Lulu to take up so much of our attention and then the cat – who never for one second was going to be down the pecking order from the dog! I do feel you have the animals in your life that you are meant to have, that there is a soul connection and you learn so much from them.'

On one occasion I stayed at Debbie's house whilst teaching and looked after Coco. She is not only stunningly beautiful but a very communicative cat, and we shared many conversations during my stay. Coco is also an accomplished healer and when I connected to her with healing energy she would reciprocate. As a result, I returned home from my busy trip invigorated and spiritually replenished.

When we see our pets in the best possible light and understand just what they can do for us, it changes our life for the better. I think it is sad when people compare one pet with another, for each has something unique and special to offer. They respond to love and that is the greatest gift that we can give, accepting them for what they are. Love and acceptance also means allowing pets the space and freedom in which to express themselves, for only then can we truly get to know them.

Flying angels and farm angels

It's fascinating how angels can adopt bird form, perhaps attracted to birds by their wings. Sue, my editor, shared a lovely magpie story with me. A friend's father freed a magpie which was tangled up in some netting in his garden. The next morning the man sat down on a bench outside in the fresh air to enjoy a cup of coffee. Suddenly the magpie swooped down and landed on his shoulder. Then it nuzzled up to him, rubbing its beak against his cheek a couple of times before flying off and disappearing out of the garden. That incident totally changed the way that Sue regards magpies. And it reminded me that birds are feathered angels.

When we are troubled, any animal can act in a way that lightens our heart. Pangiota from Greece told me how she was very upset one day and went to the place where her goats are kept. The goats were a little afraid of humans so they normally never came close to her. However, while Pangiota sat crying, one of the goats actually did approach her this time. As the goat looked into Pangiota's eyes, Pangiota clearly heard it speaking to her, asking what was wrong. Pangiota said that the goat's concern immediately made her feel better – her worries vanished into thin air. The goat, having made a soul connection, would have been able to transmit healing energy, which immediately lifts our mood.

Is there an angel in the sky, in a field, woodland or associated with water near where you live, that can improve your day?

The Muscovy duck

I first noticed the Muscovy duck when he was sitting on the roof ridge of a house across the road from where I live. A large duck on a house roof? How strange. The area has many ponds and rivers more suited to a duck and his webbed feet than a house roof. The next morning as I was eating my breakfast, my cats started making a chattering noise as they gazed up through the conservatory windows. Looking down on me from his perch on our house gable end was the duck. What on earth was a duck doing up there? I again asked myself.

A few days later, as I rushed out to get into my car for an emergency dental appointment, I noticed the duck sitting on the roof ridge of the house next door. He was cocking his head from side to side, looking at me. The penny then dropped. For a few weeks, things in my life had been going distinctly pear-shaped. Everything that possibly could go wrong had done, even catastrophically so. At a very low ebb one night, I had prayed to my guardian angels, telling them how depleted I felt, and asking if they could send a sign that my plight had been noticed. Could they help me?

It was a few days after this that the roof-sitting duck had appeared. He was my sign, an angel in the guise of a duck, no doubt reporting back to the divine source that he was keeping an eye on me. Acknowledging this, I stopped at my car door and, waving to the duck, shouted, 'Thank you, angel, for looking after me.' He watched me drive off and I felt that my turbulent few weeks would soon be coming to an end. Certainly I knew that beneficial energy was being directed at me, and that made me feel a whole lot better.

> *Animals encourage us to connect with them because it's good for the soul.*

A dog's laughter

Angel pets like to make us laugh. I look after five sheltie dogs when their owner is away; they are four females and a male called Blue, who was given his name owing to his having one brown and one blue eye. Each evening the dogs are given a couple of biscuits at bedtime, and the routine is that when I reach for the dog-biscuit tin they all pile out of the dog flap to a small table on the patio and line up for their treats.

One evening, after I had finished looking at emails on my laptop, I went to unwind by playing with the dogs. After a while I placed the treats tin on the table and counted out five biscuits. Then, placing them in the palm of my left hand, and starting with Blue, who had positioned himself at the right-hand end of the line of dogs facing me, I gave each dog a biscuit.

Except … when I got to the last dog I looked into my hand and thought, 'Oh no, I've made a mistake with counting out the biscuits. There is one dog to go and I don't have a biscuit left!'

I began to doubt my ability to count and thought that, being fatigued from computer work, I had got the numbers wrong when I had taken the biscuits out of the tin. It was nearly dark by this time, but an outside light illuminated the dogs in front of me and, as I turned to the tin to get another treat, the light glinted in the blue eye of the dog sitting in front of me. It was Blue! He had craftily nipped from one end of the queue to the other, and even crouched down a bit so that his bigger size was not so obvious as he stood next to Lilly, who is the same merle colouring as him. In the moment that I realised what was going on I noticed the look in the dog's eye … he was thinking, '*I hope she doesn't notice it's me!*'

'Blue, it's you,' I said. 'You crafty boy, I did have enough biscuits to go around after all. You nearly had me there!'

I roared with laughter at Blue's cleverness, and could sense that he found it funny too. A dog certainly does have the knack of making you forget your troubles and can bring some much needed light-heartedness to the moment.

Healing has many aspects to it and it needs to be shared, as animals ably demonstrate. The more we open a healing heart to all creatures, the more our mind can expand. The next chapter takes us into the realms of what is possible when this happens.

Angel pets make us laugh,
to remind us of their joy.

4 🐾 Pets Predict

Truth is something that pets see.

Our future hangs on a thread and I believe that animals sense this very acutely. They want to guide us forwards, which reinforces their role as our guardian angels. There are many studies which conclude that animals, as well as humans, have a sixth sense that can reveal the future. Of course, while this phenomenon has been acknowledged by many people for thousands of years, it's not a concept that is popular with scientists – the sixth sense isn't something that can be put into a test tube and examined under a microscope. To uncover the facts about the sixth sense and explore the powerful benefits of prediction we first need to acknowledge its very existence. Then, freed from embarrassment or shyness, we begin to act on our pets' premonitions, as well as on our own.

Animals have premonitions and it's undoubtedly a mystery to them why we don't see things as clearly as they do. Premonitions are impressions of something that is going to happen, often coming as a warning of a future event. I expect that many of you have had instances when you have had a 'gut feeling' or a hunch about something about to happen, and were proved right. Children especially can have this acute sensitivity, because in this respect they do not have the self-doubt of adults. Premonitions can aid our survival as a species, because they give us information about what an outcome might be from a considered action.

In some of the instances in which pets have had premonitions and therefore been able to act as guardian angels, they have provided information that encouraged someone to change their plans; on other occasions animals have known what a person was about to do, having had a premonition of their intentions.

There are many anecdotes about animals acting strangely before the 2004 Indian Ocean tsunami. One man was reported as saying that his two dogs would not to go onto the beach that day for their usual run. Normally they were excited about the outing, but on that particular occasion they refused to go and this most probably saved the man's life. Sceptics say that the animals, including elephants, dogs, cats, bats, birds and other forms of wildlife, all picked up on atmospheric energies relating to the tsunami, such as sounds or earth movements. Perhaps, but the actions of the animals described elsewhere in this chapter could not have been due to those things.

Disasters often have stories attached to them about how some people avoided being there at the time, owing to their having had an uneasy feeling beforehand. In his book *The Power of Premonitions*, Larry Dossey says that the terrorist atrocities of September 11, 2001 were preceded by a slew of premonitions. And when the *Titanic* made her fatal voyage it was reported that many passengers had a sense of foreboding. Dossey mentions the case of a woman who was driving with her cat travelling on the back seat of her car. As the woman drove along the cat became increasingly agitated, but the woman ignored its antics. Suddenly it jumped across onto the front seat and bit the woman, forcing her to stop. At that precise moment a huge tree crashed across the road, with a terrific bang. The woman was shocked because if she had continued driving she would no doubt have been killed.

Jacobena and the tree

Something similar happened to George, whose cat Jacobena I know well. George often goes for evening walks with Jacobena, who likes to be carried for these outings. One still summer evening after looking around his terrace, George turned to go up a particular garden path, Jacobena cradled in his arms. As soon as George did this, Jacobena started to wriggle and scrabble, clawing George badly.

'What's wrong?' he asked Jacobena. 'You've been carried here all your life, and never played up like this.'

Jacobena fought so defiantly that George set the cat down at his feet, whereupon she hurtled back the way they had come, with George in hot pursuit. Once Jacobena reached the other side of the house she happily mooched around that part of the garden, so George got on with tending his plants.

Some minutes later there was an explosive crash. A large oak tree had collapsed across the path that Jacobena had refused to go up. Later investigation showed that the trunk had rotted and the tree could have fallen at any time. There is no doubt in George's mind that Jacobena knew precisely when the fall of the tree was imminent. We humans will never know what signals nature emits, but this cat did ... and it helped not only save her owner, but one of her own nine lives.

Jacobena seems to have an affinity for trees because there was another incident a few years later. Around three o'clock one morning, George was woken by a storm. Both Jacobena and his other cat Gwen were on the bed with him and neither cat was bothered by the thunder and lightning, having heard it many times before. The storm had raged for about twenty minutes when suddenly Jacobena sat bolt upright and started to wail. George told me that it was unlike any sound that he had ever before heard a cat make. It was not a chatty, wanting-attention kind of noise, or a 'feed me' request, but ethereal and spooky, with an ominous air of urgency about it.

Thinking that Jacobena had something seriously wrong with her, George checked her over for signs of injury or illness, but her body seemed fine. Then Gwen joined in, making the same sound, which again sounded like an urgent distress call. Both cats seemed panicky about something and made the eerie noise half a dozen times, leaving George to wonder what on earth was going on. Suddenly there was a big flash and a bang from the storm followed by a stillness. At this, the cats stopped their wailing and settled down as if they had not just been indulging in such odd behaviour. There wasn't a further peep out of them until morning, when they demanded their breakfast.

Looking out of the window after he got up, George could see a burnt-out birch tree lying before him. The lightning during the night had struck the tree and blown it out of the ground. The penny then dropped as George realised what had been going on with his cats. They had had a premonition that the tree was going to be struck by lightning, which could have started a serious fire. How did the two cats know this? Did they somehow conjure up a force to combat the power of the lightning, to stop the damage from getting out of control? We can only speculate, but those two cats know the truth of what happened that night. As will many animals the world over, due to their extraordinary precognitive ability and awareness of evolving energy fields.

Paying attention

What was it that the cat in the car with the woman tuned into, which told it a tree was about to crash across the road?

How did Jacobena know that a tree was about to fall across the garden path or that lightning was going to strike and cause a fire? Scientists come up with all sorts of theories, including that animals sense minute vibrations in their paws which signal that something unusual is about to happen. Well, let's look at the facts in these cases. The travelling cat was in a car, and vehicles have continuous complex vibrations as they move over uneven road surfaces. That cat was prevented from hearing any rustling or creaking sounds from the tree because of the car's engine noise and, anyway, the cat started to become agitated some distance away from the scene of disaster. When Jacobena sensed that the tree was about to collapse, she was being carried – so her paw pads were not touching the ground to pick up any tremors. George, who was facing the tree when his cat started clawing to get away, did not hear anything untoward nor see the tree sway in warning. On the night of the storm when Jacobena and Gwen had started their eerie wailing, the gale had been raging for quite some time, and until that point the cats were in a relaxed state. They made their warning calls a couple of minutes before lightning struck a healthy tree.

Over the years I have learnt to pay close attention to pet behaviour in case I miss something important that they are telling me.

The horse angel

A lot of my work involves horses. Being prey animals, they rely particularly heavily on their senses to warn them of impending danger. Horses are often called 'big pets' by their owners, especially if horses become a focal part of their lives.

I live not far from a woman whose horse showed her just to what extent he is her best buddy. The horse has a reputation for being co-operative, easy to be with and safe to ride. One fine afternoon the woman got the horse ready for a ride, but for the first time ever he refused to go out of the gate onto the lane. She took the horse back to the yard and everything about him was thoroughly checked, yet nothing untoward was found. So the woman tried again, and the horse walked with her to the gate, but as before he planted his feet and refused to budge.

Turning him around, the woman led the horse to the paddock. She wondered if he was lame, but seeing that he was not, she led him back to the gate. As they reached the gate this time there was a loud roar, together with a blur of red and orange, as two speeding sports cars shot past them – young men racing each other on the country lane. It occurred to the woman that it was a good job her horse was playing up that day, because if they had been on the narrow, bendy road the cars would have ploughed into them and they would both have been killed. The woman looked up at her horse in gratitude ... who then stepped politely forward to go out of the gate.

Later the woman told everyone what had happened. Her guardian angel horse had deliberately held back from going onto the road as he knew that danger loomed. But how did he know? The cars would have been a couple of miles away when he was first asked to go out of the gate. There was nothing passing by when the horse initially refused to leave the yard. Could the horse hear the speeding cars in the distance? I don't think it was that, because this was a traffic-proof horse, used to being alongside buses and trucks. I believe that it is yet another example of an animal having a greater awareness and perception than we humans of what is going on in the world, owing to its superior sixth-sense abilities. We have a lot of ground to cover if we wish to follow in the footsteps of our animal guardians.

When we are with pets we should take extra care to notice their cues about danger. A dog who refuses to go somewhere can be pulled along – unlike a big horse – but maybe he or she is warning you about something. I always like to stop and ask. George turned back when his cat Jacobena became alarmed – and remember Twinkle, the rabbit who saved a little girl's life by urging the trapped girl's sister to follow her, knowing the peril she was in? Animals in their angel capacity know far more than we do about a lot of things, and getting into the habit of being as aware of our surroundings as they are can only be a good thing.

The factors that influenced these animals can affect us too if we remain open to them, but we are oblivious to much of the cosmic information that seems to be readily available to them. This makes us out of touch with our surroundings. Animals demonstrate time and again how acutely in tune they are with the universe, connecting through senses which we humans neglect to use. The concept of the sixth sense is often derided and so people do not always feel confident about exploring it. But practising tuning into an animal's way of receiving information could protect us from injury or even save our life.

Angel pets are always on the lookout
for ways in which they can direct our path.

Past lives

Pets sometimes show me that they have a sense of a past life, and I confess I find it especially interesting when that life has involved me!

Claude, a twelve-year-old tabby cat, was lying on the sofa; he was recovering from surgery to remove a malignant tumour from between his shoulder blades. When I walked into the room and glanced at him, Claude opened his eyes wide, and I quite clearly heard him say, 'I knew you were coming.' Simultaneously, my soul recognised this being as someone I had known before in another life ... and I thought: 'I know you.'

But Claude didn't want to chat. He was groggy from the two anaesthetics that he had had earlier that week, and just wanted some healing to help him recover and fight the cancer. Touching Claude's body felt utterly familiar to me, as though I had done this many times before. Several times Claude stretched out his legs in a happy cat way and when I got up to leave, he seemed asleep; certainly his eyes were tightly shut.

Debbie and Tony, with whom Claude lived, sent me an update on his progress a few days later. Something very interesting had happened shortly after I had left the house. Debbie was just commenting on how relaxed Claude was when he opened his eyes, jumped off the sofa and went to the door in a split second. At that moment Tony caught sight through the window of my car as it pulled away. Next Claude went to the window and, looking up, 'asked' to sit on the sill. He was not well enough to jump so Tony lifted Claude up and let him sit there, where for five minutes or so he glanced back and forth. Debbie and Tony felt sure that he was looking for me. After doing this Claude went back to the sofa and flaked out.

I am sure that Claude had a flashback, a sense of déjà vu of a shared past. Perhaps Claude, remembering me from another life, wished that I could stay, or wanted to wave goodbye. Interestingly, as I drove off I felt refreshed, as though I had just awoken from a sleep myself. Soul to soul, what had Claude and I been discussing during my visit? He knew, I am sure of that, but because I am human and there-fore a novice in the communication stakes, I did not. Some day, though, when I most need it the angelic knowledge that he infused in me will surface, to help me in whatever way it is meant to.

Debbie ended her update by saying, 'I always feel sure that Claude knows far more than me. Sometimes when he makes eye contact it feels like he is assessing you and trying to help, rather than the other way around.'

The experience with Claude reminds me of another past-life story. Liz Mitten Ryan, a Canadian horsewoman and author, was devastated when coyotes killed her whippet, Hercules. As much as Liz wanted another whippet she was afraid to have a small dog again, owing to the dangers on her ranch. Instead, Liz found a breeder of Leonbergers nearby, which are big dogs that look like lions. A litter was due in a couple of months' time, and meditating, Liz received a clear picture that one puppy would have a white sunburst shape on its chest, and would be Hercules reincarnated. Doing her chores one morning, Liz sensed Hercules with her. Phoning the breeder, Liz was told that the first puppy in the litter had just been born ... and had a white sunburst on its chest. On seeing the puppy, Liz knew instantly that Hercules had come back to her, now as a female dog which she called Ra, after the ancient Egyptian sun god.

Chichan's last day

Through a message from a pet, we may be led to have our own premonition. Sitting in a car one day, Miki from Osaka, Japan was suddenly aware of 'seeing' two budgies that she used to have called Qchan and Happy. Miki describes the vision as not like seeing a ghostly image with your eyes but like looking at the birds from within, the images projected inside her forehead.

The two spirit budgies appeared as huge images, the size of large angels, and Miki felt that they had appeared to tell her that her four-year-old pet budgie Chichan was almost ready to join them. This surprised Miki as Chichan was in good health. Following that, Miki had another vision, this time of the two spirit birds on a boat. In dream interpretation boats are recognised as symbols of a person's life. It was confirmation that Chichan was leaving.

Then Miki developed severe neck pain, which hurt so much that she had to lie down. An injection from the doctor did not help and so Miki had to cancel her schedule and stay at home for the day. Although Chichan seemed well, Miki's strong feeling about soon losing him was now so overpowering, she decided being at home was a good opportunity to spend some time with him. Opening the cage, Miki let her pet out, and by his posture and body language she could see that Chichan was asking her to play with him. Chichan was a real character, a very pretty pale blue bird who made strong eye contact with Miki as he talked to her. After Miki had played with Chichan, he asked her and her mother for a hug in the way that he used to when he was a baby bird, by pushing his head against them.

After a while Miki and her mum got out a handkerchief, something that Chichan used to have a habit of sleeping in when he was younger. Chichan hopped into it and snuggled down as Miki gently tucked the cloth around him. Then he promptly fell asleep. Reluctant to disturb Chichan, Miki placed the budgie on a cushion, which she and her Mom took turns to hold throughout the evening. At midnight, while Miki's mother held the cushion and gently watched over him, Chichan died in his sleep. He had flown into the great beyond to join the two waiting birds, which had a couple of days earlier come to prepare Miki for his departure.

The next morning Miki's neck was not hurting and she believes that Chichan had so badly wanted to spend his last day with her that she was meant to stay at home, to surround him with love as he took his last breath. Somehow – and we mere mortals will never understand how – the two spirit messenger birds had appeared to Miki so that Chichan could have his wish. We should never overlook that fact that, as well as giving love and comfort to us in abundance, all creatures – no matter how small – need these qualities from us as well. Nothing is insignificant, and everything is part of the whole.

Premonitions about Daisy

My friend Ruth was driving along when a random thought popped into her mind. 'I wonder what my husband would do if I came home with a black dog without telling him?' The thought hung in the air and, shaking her head, Ruth wondered where it had come from.

That evening, as Ruth tucked her children into bed, the telephone rang. 'I thought I'd give you a call,' said her neighbour Sandra. 'The thing is, a couple of our friends are emigrating to Australia but they have an elderly black Labrador, Daisy. A member of the family was going to have her, but has suddenly died. Is there any chance that you might take Daisy on?'

Ruth telephoned the dog's owners, who assured her that they had already found a home for Daisy. Ruth knew, though, that Daisy would soon be joining her own family. Sure enough, a couple of days later she received a phone call to say that the foster family had withdrawn their offer.

Daisy arrived at Ruth's house on a Sunday morning, and the people who brought her there were clearly distressed at the thought of leaving her. There were angels around, however, including one who helped Ruth's six-year-old son draw a picture of Daisy surrounded by bones – just the type that any dog might dream of eating. When the picture was pinned over Daisy's bed in the corner of Ruth's kitchen, the dog wandered over and hopped into the basket as though it had always been her place.

Ruth only had to look at Daisy to be flooded with peace and calm. Her influence proved to be a special gift when a couple of years later Ruth found herself pregnant with her third child and struggling to cope with the stress of having builders around the house. Although Ruth knew that Daisy would not live much longer, she also knew the dog would remain until the birth.

On the day that Ruth went into labour, Daisy fell ill. With her usual enthusiasm, faithful Daisy welcomed Ruth's baby daughter, as well as helping Ruth cope with the early hectic days of motherhood. It was Daisy's final blessing on the family before she passed away three weeks later.

Departing souls

Pets often seem to have a natural ability to know when a person is about to pass away. Kathy used to work in a care home and she told me about a cat there called Ginger who could predict death. Ginger had been in a rescue shelter before he was adopted by the care home owners, so he had a great time exploring the woods that surrounded the care home. When Ginger came indoors and started to make a beeline for someone's room – which was sometimes several times a day – and then lie on the bed, the staff knew that it was an ominous sign. Invariably within a few days that person would pass away. So when the cat did this, the nurses would encourage the relatives to make as many visits as possible, knowing that time was running out.

Ginger was in contact with the people who were passing, but other animals may be in a completely different place and still sense a departing soul. After a terrible storm one night, Marianne and her husband were woken by their two cats Pen and Gizmo, who were howling, meowing and generally making the most terrible noise, whilst running around the bedroom. The curtains billowed and snapped due to the wind raging outside, and at first Marianne thought the cats' odd behaviour was due to the storm. A few minutes later the telephone rang. It was Marianne's brother to say that their father had just died. Marianne is convinced that the cats knew this before the phone rang, as they have never behaved that way before, or since.

Sometimes a pet a person used to have returns in spirit form as a reassuring presence as the soul prepares to leave the body. When my mother was recovering in hospital after a hip fracture, she suddenly started to talk about our childhood dog Patch, who she said was sitting on the edge of her bed and looking at her. She was aware that the dog had died many years earlier and told us that he had come back as a spirit to watch over her. I knew it wasn't the ramblings of an old lady, but an omen. Patch, as angels often do, had come as a messenger of death and sure enough my mother unexpectedly passed away two days later, with Patch by her side to lead the way to her everlasting home.

Telepathic dogs

Premonitions needn't be about impending death or disaster, and can be intriguing. There was an occasion once, whilst communicating with a dog, when I picked up the image of a book. The dog's owner had not lost a book or been given a book; in fact she was not a keen reader. Every time I said that I could see this book hovering in the mind of the dog and that it seemed somehow to symbolise joy, he would sigh. I know from experience that this can be a sign that a pet is agreeing with information I am passing on. He must have felt frustrated, though, because his message was impossible for us to interpret.

Several weeks later the woman called me. 'You'll never guess what came in the mail this morning,' she gasped. 'A book!' It was not a normal book, however, but a paperback which had been hollowed out in the middle. Nestling inside the space was a small brooch in the shape of a butterfly.

A few weeks earlier the woman had seen this piece of jewellery at a craft fair, but could not afford to buy it. By some strange quirk of fate her sister, who lived in another town, had seen the item when the jewellery-maker attended a sale in her area. Knowing that it was the sort of thing that her sister would like, she bought it to cheer her up and posted it inside a discarded paperback. How did the dog know that this would happen? I got the feeling that he expected me to know how it could be done. It was no big deal as far as he was concerned to be a clairvoyant dog.

Dogs often demonstrate an uncanny knack of predicting what someone is about to do. Dr Marcie Fallek, a holistic New York vet, told me how she used to leave her dog Savannah, an Australian sheepdog/sheltie mix, at an elderly couple's house when she worked away or went on vacation. They would tell Marcie how uncanny it was that exactly ten minutes before she came to pick Savannah up, the dog would restlessly keep going to the door. Savannah was waiting for Marcie and it didn't matter where she was coming from, by which mode of transport or how long she had been away – the dog always knew when she was about to arrive.

Carol runs a busy London riding school and her doggy best friend is Benji, a sable-coloured German shepherd. Benji knows Carol's intention before she makes a move to carry it out. In the evenings, after a day with horses, Carol relaxes in front of the TV, or reads whilst Benji sprawls out on his bed. A lot of things go through Carol's mind as the TV plays or she flicks through magazines and books, including what went on during the day, people to telephone, meetings to attend, family to visit.

Without fail, if Carol decides she needs to go out in her car, Benji will immediately get up and go to the front door. He has a particular love of car journeys. Carol will most probably be staring at the TV screen or a magazine page when the thought crosses her mind, and she won't have given Benji any clues such as reaching for her car keys to alert him to her intention. It doesn't matter whether Carol has decided to go somewhere in the car where it's impossible to take Benji, he still goes to the door. But if Carol thinks about going down to the stables or outside to fetch something, Benji doesn't move from his bed.

Benji has illustrated his mind-reading ability even from another room to the one that Carol was in. Finishing her tea, Carol looked at the bit of chicken left on her plate and thought to herself, *'Benji would like this.'* Sitting prettily by Carol's feet was her cat, so Carol decided that she should have the titbit instead. As Carol bent to put her plate on the floor for her purring puss, Benji bounded up the stairs into the kitchen, a room he never enters when Carol is eating. Benji knew that Carol was thinking of giving him something tasty to eat, so he arrived full of anticipation. When Benji saw the cat tucking in to the chicken, he looked very forlorn and, turning around, sorrowfully retraced his steps.

Carol tells me she knows what Benji is thinking because his thoughts are transmitted directly to her soul, which means she actually has them inside her – what he wants, needs, how he feels. It is as though they are her own experiences. This, of course, will be similar to how Benji tunes into Carol, a perfect example of a deep bond.

Marianne, an artist friend from New York, described to me how her childhood family dog could anticipate actions. Simone, a toy collie dog, would invariably be asleep in the bedroom when Marianne's father was watching TV, but if he suddenly decided to have a sweet the dog would wake up and come into the room with her nose twitching, pointing at the candy jar. It happened so frequently that it became a family joke.

My clairvoyant cat

Putting my hand up to my throat, the necklace that I always wore was missing. Looking around, I saw the pendant part in the middle of the floor, which was strange because I had spent a couple of hours sprawled in an armchair, reading. The gold chain, however, was nowhere to be seen.

I searched the house, moving items around in case the chain had fallen behind something, but drew a blank. The cat living with me at the time was Casey, and he wandered around observing me scrutinise rooms. I was in a difficult transition period in my life and for a few weeks had had several incidents of angels moving objects around my house, in their effort to let me know that they were around, and to have faith for a better future. For this reason I knew that an angel was responsible for removing my jewellery, but where had it been put?

Passing a large pot plant upstairs, I noticed how dusty it was, and so took the opportunity to take it into the bathroom and give the leaves a good wash and polish before putting it back. Fed up and tired, I went back downstairs to have a think. As I sat down, Casey sprang onto my lap. 'Where on earth has that chain got to?' I asked him.

'It's on a leaf on the big plant.'

'Don't be ridiculous,' I scoffed. 'I've just moved the plant, washed all the leaves, put it back again and there is nothing on it.'

Casey repeated his message.

So I got up and went back upstairs … and, sure enough, draped across a leaf was my chain. It was totally impossible for this to be so, yet it was there. To this day I am intrigued about what exactly happened. One of my guardian angels came by and Casey, as an angel pet, thought that it was all perfectly normal. No doubt he thought that I was out of kilter with the facts of the matter, so he gave me a clue as to what was going on.

Animals appear to function in a dimension that humans only occasionally skirt around. Every now and again I get a tantalising glimpse into the 'bigger picture' through tuning into a pet. I often wonder why animals are privileged to have an advanced consciousness in terms of the psychic sense. When they operate on this level they are not seeing, or sensing, something that does not exist, but something very real. Animals encourage me to want to know more about their extraordinary powers, including communicating from a distance – a topic I delve into in the next chapter.

*Every time we sense that
'something is going on', it is!*

5 Lost and Found

There are no boundaries.
You can talk to a pet anywhere, any time.

Animals naturally understand that energy fields are part of the giant communication network. It's like the internet or a telephone system, except you don't need a computer or phone to send and receive messages. Using our sixth sense, we can link to pets when we are not with them, as they can to us. One of the things that angels and pets have in common is that they can communicate with us from a distance and always know what is going on. But it's not exclusive to pets – we can also share in this process.

You may already have had an experience whereby you sensed that you were connecting with a pet that you were not actually with. The animal may have been in a cattery or kennels, a veterinary hospital, at home whilst you were elsewhere or with someone else. This sensation would be because the animal was sending you a message. They really do like to keep in touch.

You can activate sending a message to a pet by deliberately tuning into him or her. Messages can include sending love, support, comfort, information that you are on your way to collect the animal or returning home, and so on. Through telepathy we can also link with lost pets, as well as the spirit of an animal that has passed away.

When I have been consulted for an animal, particularly more than once, it is not uncommon for him or her to connect with me in times of need. Jessie, a collie cross, had been for X-rays which meant her having a general anaesthetic. Owing to numerous health problems she was particularly reactive to the drugs, but at the time I was not aware of this. On the day that Jessie went to the clinic I was standing in my kitchen when I sensed her presence with me. I had the impression that Jessie felt dreadful and was asking for healing to be sent, which I did. Looking up at the clock I noticed that it was 5 p.m. When I contacted the owner to mention this, she told me that Jessie had arrived home from the vets at exactly that time and crashed out on her bed. An hour later she got up, seemingly much perkier, and asked for something to eat. When I visited a few days later, Jessie curled onto my lap like a child instinctively going to its mother for help to recover from an ordeal.

Poppy, a year-old cream Labrador, was another dog who would 'call me'. She had several health problems related to irresponsible breeding, including hip dysplasia and seizures. As if that was not bad enough, Poppy then developed a brain tumour. Poppy was Baba and Mahmoud's first dog, and they took great care to select a breeder who was registered, and who they could visit, believing that way they would get a healthy puppy. Baba and Mahmoud told me how their hearts were later broken when they learned about breed flaws encouraged by show-ring standards, and inbreeding owing to drawing on a too-small gene pool. These things affect quality of life, and affected animals suffer all manner of distressing and painful conditions. There needs to be a shift in emphasis away from status and the looks of dogs and cats, towards improved health and temperament. Animals with problems should not be bred from, but too often that is not the case. People pay substantial sums for pedigrees and there is a great emotional investment too as the pet becomes a much-loved member of the family. It becomes a distressing scenario all round. A very caring couple, Baba and Mahmoud doted on Poppy, though, holding her paw through health struggles, and giving her the best of everything.

Shortly after my second visit to the home, Poppy linked with me early one afternoon. After I had contacted Baba and Mahmoud to ask about what was going on with the dog, they emailed in reply: 'Poppy has had a rough few days, so we are not surprised that she spoke to you today. But tonight she has picked up a lot.' It began to follow a pattern, with Poppy frequently coming into my mind and my sending her healing thoughts. Whenever I contacted Baba and Mahmoud to say that Poppy had 'called me', it always coincided with her having a bad day. After I sent healing thoughts, Poppy would then perk up.

Cats, of course, cannot be left out, as they are very good communicators from a distance. I was tuning into Sammy, a very sick moggy, when I sensed his life-force energy slip away. He was still communicating with me, but I knew he had left his body. Sure enough, when I checked with his carer, Sammy had gone outside to find a place to die. The woman took great comfort from the fact that Sammy was still able to continue sending soul-to-soul messages.

🐾 A Helping Paw

🐾 If you are away from home, or your pet is elsewhere for some reason, you can still keep in touch. Send regular mind-to-mind 'news reports' – thoughts about what you are doing and when you will next be with the pet.

🐾 If an animal comes into your mind it is sending you a message. In return send love and good wishes so that he or she can take what is needed.

When angels go missing

I am often contacted by desperate people in the hope that I may be able to pick up on the whereabouts of a missing cat or dog. It's a horrible situation to be in. Casey once went out and didn't return home for his supper. Knowing something was amiss I walked the streets, calling his name, a sinking feeling in my heart. At about midnight I went home to meditate on the problem and after a while I sensed that Casey was not far away, my mind drawn to a particular area of the town. It was a street that I had already searched, twice in fact, and it also came to me that my cat had been calling out as I walked past but his voice was too faint to be heard.

I returned to the street and was drawn to a row of garages. As I was approaching the fourth one along, the hairs on the back of my neck stood on end – I sensed my cat was inside it. Pressing my ear to the garage door I heard the faintest meow. Thankfully the door opened when I pulled at the handle. A very scared Casey was sitting on a beam over the door, covered in cobwebs. It was a huge relief for both of us to be reunited and, as we hugged, he purred the loudest that I had ever heard. We were lucky, for I found out later that the property owners were leaving for a two-week holiday early the next morning and would have locked the garage before they left, thinking that all was in order. They had put some boxes in it earlier in the day and had not noticed my curious cat sneak in behind them to investigate the nooks and crannies.

Difficulties with finding missing pets

Almost all professional animal communicators find dealing with lost animals the most challenging aspect of their work. Sometimes people say to me, 'If animals are so clever, and have this sixth sense ability, why then can't they find their way back home?' One of the reasons is that we have created an electrical fog in our technical world, which is also filled with man-made structures, all of which confuse scent trails. Another reason is that lost animals may be trapped, injured or deceased – although that in itself is no barrier to their sending us messages.

Chatting to Carol Gurney, author of *The Language of Animals – 7 Steps to Communicating with Animals* and founder of the Gurney Institute of Animal Communication, I learned that communicating with lost animals is one of her particular specialities. I wanted to hear how she approached it so I asked her: 'Why is it so difficult to tune into missing pets?' This is Carol's fascinating reply:

When an animal is lost, it can be very difficult to distinguish the animal's thoughts about where he'd like to be or what he's seen on his journey from his images of his actual physical surroundings. Imagine sunning yourself on the beach and dreaming about your winter ski vacation in the mountains – what a confusing impression of your whereabouts your thoughts would give anyone who tuned into you telepathically. They would get an image of you skiing while you were very happily sitting right on the beach. That's just one of the difficulties that lost animal communication poses.

It can be extremely difficult to ascertain whether the animal is still in a physical body or not. When an animal has met with sudden death, perhaps by the impact of a car or an attack by another animal, he may not be aware he's out of his physical body – it has happened too fast. So, when someone gets in touch with this animal, the animal may show where he is and what is around him, not recognising that he is experiencing these things in spirit form rather than in physical form.

The reverse of this situation can also happen. When an animal is extremely frightened, the communication received can feel as if he has left his body even though he is very much alive. And in a sense, he has been literally scared out of his wits because the terror is so uncomfortable to deal with. The person contacting him can mistakenly interpret that state of fear. The person trying to connect with this animal might get blankness and feel that means the animal must be out of the body. But that has been proven wrong to me. It can just indicate that the animal is extremely frightened and is unreachable at that time, and so you want to return again and see if you can calm the animal down a bit to see if a connection can be made to ascertain the truth about the situation. I have found that the appropriate question to ask an animal is 'are you still in your physical body?' versus asking 'are you still alive?' If you ask the animal if he is still alive, and if the animal has moved onto spirit form, he is still 'alive'. So I discovered the better question to ask is 'are you still in your physical body?' because that is the truth you are seeking. Sometimes, it's quite evident that the animal is in the body and other times it is unclear. When there is a lack of clarity, then I have developed several techniques that can be used to ascertain, as close as possible, the reality of the situation.

Then we have the issue of determining, if the animal is still in the body, whether the animal is truly lost. Sometimes they are not. Quite often, an animal has left home for a reason that may not be negotiable. Sometimes the animal is simply seeking adventure, or looking for a new home because they feel they've completed their job with the family. Sometimes they leave because of dissatisfaction with their present situation, and some leave to die knowing that their people are very uncomfortable with the issue of death. Some animals are truly lost because they've been stolen or chased by another animal, or have run away when frightened by something without paying attention to their surroundings.

All of these situations contribute to the challenges in finding lost animals. There are some animal communicators who have chosen not to include this service in their profession but with practice, determination, and great attention to detail, it can be a heart-warming and rewarding experience to help families come together again.

Because of the amount of travelling that I do, I am unable to take on consultations for missing pets, but I do offer help to friends, such as the time when I got a call from my German agent, Doris.

Locating Rusty

I knew that Doris had acquired a new dog – her old Polish terrier had succumbed to heart failure and after a period of mourning she discussed with her vet the idea of offering a home to a dog in need. A short while later the vet contacted Doris to say that a couple had brought in a three-year-old rough collie/border collie crossbreed called Rusty, and for personal reasons they had to let him go.

Doris and her partner Nic Raine, renowned composer and conductor of the Prague City Orchestra, fell for Rusty as soon as they went to see whether he was suitable for them. Rusty showed them that he was a friendly, playful character so they took him home to meet their five horses and cat, Balu. Rusty settled in immediately, and the horses thought he was fun, although it would take Balu a while to be totally relaxed about the idea of having a big dog running around. Balu has never relinquished his status as being in charge, and Rusty soon came to realise that.

Five days after Rusty had arrived at his new home I received an email from Doris that Rusty had run away – she was naturally distraught and asked me if I could help her. The details of what exactly had happened emerged during a phone call later. Rusty had been playing in the fields and a couple in a neighbouring property had been talking to him from over their low garden wall. The dog ran towards them to make a physical contact and despite their warning shout to stay away he leapt up at the wall and immediately received an electric shock. They kept cows and had placed an electric fence along the wall so the cows would not lean over to eat flowers from their garden.

Rusty screamed horrifically and then ran, bolting into the distance as fast as he could to get away from the source of so much pain. He was in no state to listen to Doris pleading with him to come back, and disappeared from view. For hours Doris and Nic scoured the surrounding countryside, searching woods, fields, ponds and farms. The next day Doris rode one of her horses for miles, all the time hoping that there may be a sighting of him, but there was no sign of Rusty. His previous owners were contacted in case he returned to them, vets informed should someone hand the dog in, and posters put up. Doris cried so much that when she went to meetings she had to wear dark sunglasses to cover her puffy red eyes.

Whenever I tried to reach Rusty telepathically I drew a blank – he was not listening to me; in shock he seemed to have switched off his 'radar'. Then I sensed him by a single-storey building where he was foraging for food. Days went by and I could not pick anything up. I tried again one evening, lighting a candle, as staring at a flame helps us to clear our mind and focus on our thoughts. Concentrating, I then sent a message to Rusty in the hope that he could hear me. Could he tell me where he was? The place in my mind where I would expect to receive information from the dog was empty. He was not in communication with me, and by this time Doris and Nic feared the worst – that Rusty had been shot by a farmer or hit by a vehicle. If so, how could they ever get over this tragedy?

The next morning I awoke at around seven and felt Rusty's presence with me. He was alive! Not only could I sense this, I could see him in my mind's eye – a mostly black dog with a long pointed head. Up to this time I had not seen a photo of Rusty but I just knew that this was him. The dog was thin and standing panting and exhausted in a grassy clearing in the middle of a dense wood.

I sent a message. 'Rusty, I see you, I hear you. Can you hear *me*?'

I saw the dog's head turn to look about as he picked up the energy from my words. Then the communication flowed between us like ricocheting bullets. I asked where he had been and he showed me seemingly endless trees. What had he eaten, was he thirsty? A little carrion but there was plenty of water in streams and ponds. What had he been doing? He had run for miles after the incident and was now completely lost. Where had he been for the past five days? Crossing woods and farmland in a depressed and fearful state, sleeping a bit but mostly wandering and trying to pick up scent trails that he recognised.

Then it was as though I was looking at Google Maps and I became orientated with where Rusty was in relation to Doris and Nic's property. He was to the east and it seemed not many miles away from safety, welcome kisses and a good meal.

'Turn around, Rusty, and run west,' I said, then imagined attaching a beam of light between him and his home. Over and over I concentrated on this link and asked that Rusty follow it. I sent an email to Doris, explaining that Rusty had been with me and we had talked. Three hours later she called me: 'Rusty is back!' She and Nic had been very sad that morning to wake again with no dog to greet them, but later, on opening the front door, were amazed to find Rusty sitting there, weak but otherwise unharmed. It was marvellous news.

Some months later I visited after a book launch in Germany and recognised Rusty immediately as the dog that I had 'seen' and helped guide home. When I greeted him he had a puzzled look in his eyes, and I sensed that he was wondering where we had met before. To help out I recalled the image of a dog lost in woods and how we met there through the angel network. Rusty responded by leaping up and playfully placing a paw on each of my shoulders, before licking my nose – it was a grateful doggy hug. During my visit I was able to share some of Rusty's magic during long walks, games and just sitting with him by my side.

Pooling our resources

Being a Border terrier and living in the country, Frodo is always getting into scrapes; in fact, over the years he has been cat-like in using up several lives. Frodo has become stuck in hedges and holes on a few occasions, but someone has always heard his whimpering and set free him.

This time, however, Frodo had been missing for several days. He had last been seen running around a field with his companion Holly as the horses were collected. Normally the dogs would follow the horses back to the stables but on this occasion Holly returned and Frodo did not. That evening Amanda and her husband Ian searched in the pitch darkness, walking along the dense hedgerows, which were peppered underneath with large animal holes. They repeatedly called

Frodo's name, stopping to listen for a noise that would indicate where he was, but there was no response. Their vigil continued with every member of the family looking for Frodo, and as the days went by the situation looked more and more hopeless.

On the evening of the sixth day I drove over. As I parked in front of a barn I looked up at the sky and sent up a plea to my own guardian angels: 'If Frodo is alive, guide him back home.'

Several of us set off to where Frodo had last been seen and searched everywhere we could access, cutting back undergrowth and digging. We worked in silence apart from calling out 'Frodo' and listening for something that might indicate a trapped animal. I sensed areas where Frodo had been, and there was one such place where Holly became very excited, throwing herself into a large hole and wagging her tail.

As time went on I started to see an image in my mind's eye of Frodo but he was weak and drowsy. I sent out a thought: 'Wake up, Frodo, and find the strength to find your way home.' As I did with Rusty, I sent a beam of light to reach Frodo, and prayed that it would help him.

It started to get dark and we were all covered in mud, for it had been raining heavily for several days, so we abandoned the search. When I left I took some photos of Frodo with me and, putting them under my pillow that night, repeated my mantra: 'If Frodo is alive, guide him back home.'

The phone rang just after breakfast. It was Amanda: 'Guess who came back this morning?'

'No!' I said. 'Frodo?'

Apparently he had been found sitting by the gate; he was wet, filthy dirty and covered in ticks. He also had several wounds and one of his back legs was rubbed raw – consistent with his having struggled to set himself free from somewhere. The first thing Frodo did was demand food, lots of it, before drinking some milk left out for the cat. When water was offered he was not interested, probably because he has been drinking rainwater for several days.

Ian mentioned later that when he had been standing next to me as we searched, he suddenly had a strong impression of 'an evil tree'. Ian is a mathematics teacher and not given to flights of fancy, and so I think that through his sixth sense he was seeing the roots of the tree which had trapped Frodo. The group of us who turned out that night had all contributed to Frodo's return by our combined energy. In effect in an almighty effort, we brought our angels together to help bring Frodo safely back.

❦ A Helping Paw

❦ If a pet is missing try sending out a beam of energy from the top of your head so that, if alive, the pet receives a 'boost' to help guide it home.

❦ When we combine in a team effort, this will enhance beneficial energy, and the communication lines become stronger. Because of this I always recommend that when people are searching for a lost pet, they gather as many people as they can to send out thoughts as a group. This becomes a powerful signal and can be a lifeline for an animal in helping it to return, if possible.

Mijbil's extreme effort

Animals can even communicate with us during the very stressful experience of trying to make their way back home after a trauma; however, when we feel intense emotion this may block us from sensing messages from a pet, owing to our feeling overwhelmed. The paradox is that intense emotion can also heighten our senses, which means that if we remain open to unseen energies we can often pick up information from missing pets.

I have known Mijbil, a pure black cat, and her owner, Roly, for just over six years since I was introduced to them by my colleague Amanda Sutton, a renowned veterinary physiotherapist and author. Amanda had been consulted to help Mijbil with lameness issues and during my first meeting with Mijbil and Roly the story of what had happened to cause this condition unfolded.

One day Mijbil had gone missing. It was not unusual for her to be out all day, exploring smells and hunting in the undergrowth as well as on the common behind the house, but it was very out of character for her not to return in the evening. Roly was concerned but thought that his cat would return during the night, perhaps greeting him with a mouse or rat as a present and letting it run around the bedroom.

The next morning came and Mijbil had still not appeared, so as the day wore on Roly became more and more concerned and agitated. Now very worried, he searched high and low, checking all around the neighbourhood, and generally looking in all the places that his cat liked to go. As night fell he experienced the devastating fear of an owner who has lost a pet. *She's gone, she's dead,* he thought to himself, *killed by either an animal or a human.* The long night was very disturbed because of that haunting thought.

A further search on waking proved fruitless and with a sinking heart Roly walked to the edge of his garden, where he sat down at a place where Mijbil liked to rest. He was going to say goodbye, to send his grief and thoughts out into the universe to reach Mijbil wherever she was, and to wish her peace. As he was thinking about his cat, Roly suddenly had the knowledge – his inner voice stating it to him as a fact – that she was *not* dead. Simultaneously he heard another voice that he intuitively knew to be that of Mijbil say, '*I'm alive. I'm here.*'

These messages were so strong that Roly did not doubt them at all, and he immediately got up to start searching again. *Where was she?* Frustratingly, the search proved fruitless once more. Day after day, Roly scoured the area carefully like a tracker, lifting low branches, poking in bushes, parting long grass, and looking down holes. Nothing. At first he was buoyed up by the messages of hope that he had received, but as time went on Roly worried that Mijbil was lying injured somewhere and that he would not reach her in time to give her whatever help she needed. If she was alive she obviously could not get back home, so how could she survive for much longer, he wondered?

Listening to less than encouraging comments from associates that his cat could not have survived for so long had she been injured, Roly began to lose hope and doubt the feelings that he was getting. Then he had a vivid dream: Mijbil was bawling at him in indignation, like she would when being ignored and trying to attract his attention. On waking, having sensed Mijbil so vibrantly in his dream, Roly resolved to carry on his search. It was eleven days after Mijbil had gone missing and suddenly Roly had a strong impression that she was not far away.

He could have gone to look in many places but he set off in the direction that his intuition guided him to follow, across a grassy bank towards some trees. Initially, Roly saw nothing. Concentrating hard, he then heard the faintest animal noise coming from the base of a fallen tree. At first Roly thought it was his other cat, Guinevere, hunting, but then he realised that she was in fact behind him. With his heart now racing Roly peered into the tree bowl and there, lying tangled in the upturned roots, was Mijbil. She was clearly in a bad way.

Very weak and unable to move, she was trying to meow but her voice was hoarse and the sound indistinct. On picking her up, Roly could see horrific wounds to Mijbil's back legs and paws. Furthermore, he noticed that the only limb that had any movement was her right front leg. With extreme urgency Roly drove to the vet for help, luckily only ten minutes away.

The vet diagnosed a stroke and said that Mijbil was paralysed and on the verge of death. Her shocking wounds were the result of her dragging herself home along the ground from the place where she had collapsed, using the one leg that she still had movement in. That massive survival effort had taken her the numerous days during which she had been missing.

The vet put Mijbil onto a drip, saying that there was little hope and that Roly should go home and wait for a phone call, but not to expect Mijbil to make it through the night. However, after all that Mijbil had been through, and given her desperate effort to reach home, Roly wasn't going to abandon her now. She needed his loving support. Much to the vet's obvious displeasure a spare room was reluctantly found where Mijbil could lie with her medical equipment and Roly could sit through the night, watching over her and praying for a miracle. During that vigil, amazingly, Roly heard Mijbil again communicate to him, stating her wish to live.

The next morning, although Mijbil was a little brighter and some movement was returning to her left front leg as well as the right, the vet said that the situation was still hopeless and advised euthanasia. Whilst he did not want his beloved cat to suffer, Roly wanted to try everything that was possible to help her.

'What else can I do in terms of rehabilitation?' he asked the vet, who stated that veterinary physiotherapy might be an option but he wasn't optimistic about the outcome. And that was how Roly arrived at Amanda's clinic for her expertise.

Happily, Mijbil has recovered the full use of her front limbs and become free from pain, although she remains compromised in her back legs. She is such a feisty, cheerful cat that it has not curbed her enjoyment of life, and her dedicated owner undertakes physiotherapy exercises with her every single day. Roly figures that as Mijbil fought to live and to come home, he will help her as long as it is the right thing to do, and she is enjoying a good quality of life and is not uncomfortable. Mijbil is also of course monitored by the holistic team.

I asked Roly if he ever found out where Mijbil's stroke happened and he told me that there is a place up on the common where he feels very uncomfortable. He senses too that Mijbil remembers it as the spot where she was in big trouble. It is an area that Roly had actually searched many times whilst Mijbil was missing, but with several acres of dense bracken he had obviously missed catching sight of her tucked deep in the tangled undergrowth.

After initially passing out, Mijbil must have been conscious when she sent Roly the message that morning, '*I am alive.*' It was this powerful and clear communication from his cat that drove Roly on, urging him not to give up and to keep looking. Mijbil in turn sensed that Roly was linking to her and she found the unbelievable strength to drag herself back to be reunited with him. That miraculous experience daily inspires Roly to do everything he can to make Mijbil's life as happy and fulfilling as can be. While he may have been Mijbil's guardian angel in her time of need, Roly feels that she now fulfils that role for him. Since Roly began to understand how to interact with Mijbil on a spiritual plane, he feels that she has been teaching him much so that he can benefit from her extraordinary wisdom.

There is no doubt that we have much to learn from all animals, and being apart from them does not break the communication link. We can influence pets from a distance, and remain interconnected with them even from far away. It's not that we are on the threshold of discovering something new in this respect; rather that we are going back to our roots and rekindling our innate skills.

We connect to pets through love.
Our love turns them into angels.

6 Wild Voices

*Take inspiration from nature's angels
so that they can nurture you.*

Outside our homes are millions of creatures going about their lives in their wild beauty, often in complete secret and out of our sight. All of these creatures communicate with each other as well as with other life forms. The animals, birds and insects that live in the wild also talk to us. They assume that we pick up their messages and understand how they relate to our planet, as well as to the universe as a whole.

When I discussed the role that animals play in our lives with American behavioural ecologist and interspecies communication specialist Mary Ann Simonds, she explained: 'Where once all people talked with the animals and honoured them for their contributions to the living system, we have now isolated them into categories of how they relate to us – such as pets, wildlife, pests, food animals, working animals and exotics, etc.'

Embracing all creatures as equally valuable teachers, healers and angel messengers will enhance our own lives in so many different ways – as the following stories show.

When we connect with nature things can happen that are very unusual, to say the least. Such occurrences may show us how insignificant we are in terms of our being in control of events, yet at the same time they reveal how much nature knows and understands each one of us in great detail. It's an old saying but very true – we are all part of the rich tapestry of life.

Given the freedom to do so, animals will express their own agendas, but they can also show an unselfish concern for others when the need arises. There are occasions when an animal may reach out to another species to make them part of their family, and that of course includes us. The basic needs of both humans and animals boil down to the same thing – survival. The difference between life and death can be determined by the assistance a creature in need receives from others, and that help can come in the form of an animal angel. Sometimes we humans take on an angel role and help a wild animal through our love of all life forms. But whenever we or an animal give love, it is always reciprocal, and the giver receives it back magnified thousands of times. That is why angels are depicted as bright celestial beings, radiating and beaming light.

There are numerous cases in which animals have taken on a caring role for other species, or formed unusual friendships. Over the years I have had cats cuddle up to rabbits, watched cats play with fox cubs, seen dogs sharing a bed with bird friends, and witnessed both cats and dogs bond with wildlife or exotic animals. On my travels around the world I have often heard about animals taking care of others in need, including dogs who greet rescued deer, rabbits, cats, birds, guinea pigs or badger cubs at shelters with a welcoming lick. This takes the stress out of the new arrivals and helps them to settle in to their surroundings. I have also seen cats mothering orphaned baby bunnies.

My cats are used to dog patients visiting, and over the years they have seen many breeds – from tiny to huge. When a dog is brought to me and it is suffering from intense emotional turmoil, my cat Teddy invariably makes a beeline for him or her, sometimes touching noses, and at other times settling down to lie close to the dog. When this happens, Teddy is giving out love and healing.

Humans have a lot to learn from animals when it comes to giving love to any creature in need. These animal 'soul caretakers' would make ideal mascots for the United Nations. They show us the healing implications of co-mingling with respect and grace, irrespective of species. It is the heart-to-heart connection that is vital when reaching out to others, whilst the soul is the master communicator – eliminating all boundaries. Animals teach and show us this, when we listen.

Nature puts on a show

Animals have brought people and opportunities into my life that I could not have encountered otherwise. Through my work I have visited the US many times, including being invited to the stunningly beautiful Rocking C's ranch in Montana to attend a unique horseman's week. It was inspirational to meet famous horsemen and horsewomen from the US and Europe, who were gathered together to promote the welfare of horses as well as to explore ideas for future events.

It was my first visit to a ranch and so I found the whole experience utterly fascinating. During time free from lectures and demonstrations I walked for miles, admiring the huge rock outcrops below which aspen trees grew, their delicate leaves fluttering in the early summer breeze. During these outings I came across a beaver dam and swallows nesting in the side of a cliff, as well as a mule deer leading her day-old fawn down a grassy slope. It was all so achingly beautiful and I took lots of photos, even though a camera can't do justice to such big scenery. Those memories can only exist inside you.

I was aware that generations ago the land had been populated by Native American Indians and I could envision these people crossing the valleys in the summer as they brought their horses to graze the lush pastures. The ranch owners are very environmentally respectful and so the land and its resources are protected and unpolluted. Remnants of tepee foundations still exist and I couldn't help but feel like a pioneer as I strolled up to the top of a hill to survey a snow-capped mountain range in the distance.

One day the ranch guests were promised a treat: a special guest would join us for the evening. So it was that I met the amazing Phillip Whiteman Jr and his paint pony Sioux Boy, with whom Phillip demonstrates ancient teachings based on the Medicine Wheel Model. Phillip is a Northern Cheyenne Indian and has similar views to me about horses belonging to the horse nation, being our mirror, and that all life is connected. It was an honour to be seated next to him at supper and, as I talked with this spiritually advanced yet modest man, I was struck by his empathy with all species and his love of nature. It oozed out of him and our conversation was over too soon, yet in that short time I learned much from this kindred spirit.

After supper I joined the other guests as we gathered by the spectacular Smith River that flows across the property. Rows of chairs had been set out on the bank facing upriver, and we were told to make ourselves comfortable for we were going to listen to Native American storytelling by Phillip. It was a perfectly still June evening and he arrived to take his place before us, having changed out of jeans and cowboy shirt into traditional clothing. In his gentle manner, Phillip first of all described the significance of his robes, particularly the colours in them, which we were told represented all the hues of the rainbow and what this meant to the tribes.

I couldn't believe my eyes when I saw what happened next: a real rainbow suddenly appeared in the sky behind Phillip, arcing majestically over the silvery-coloured river. There were audible gasps as the guests noticed it and started to nudge each other in amazement. As we marvelled, the bright rainbow hung in the sky while Phillip continued his story.

He then talked about the three eagle feathers in his head-dress, and how significant they are to his people, because for hundreds of years Native Americans have used eagle feathers for religious and cultural purposes. He told us that the eagle is a symbol of truth, power and freedom – things that are important in life. Its wings represent the balance needed between male and female, each one dependent on the strengths, attributes and abilities of the other. Just as Phillip spoke these words, a bald eagle appeared flying silently over his head and past our group, following the contour of the river.

How much better can this get? I thought to myself, and I was so overwhelmed that for a moment or too I felt quite emotional. The eagle drifted along the river towards the rainbow and gave a sensational display, silhouetted under the shape and colours. Then it turned and, circling above and around us, soared effortlessly and silently on the air currents. As it looked down with its incredible eyesight, the eagle could identify each one of us in infinite detail. I felt that this was symbolic of the source of all life knowing each one of us as a unique being.

Having treated us to his masterful display the eagle then again headed along the river and this time continued into the distance. The rainbow was fading now and Phillip sang and danced a little before recounting another tale about a duck. I turned to look at the river, astonished to see a mother duck come paddling along followed by a brood of ducklings! We were all amazed. This really was too good to be true.

After Phillip finished his performance people went up to thank him and say how much in awe they were at what had transpired. They asked whether he had physically seen the rainbow, eagle or ducks. Philip could have claimed great supernatural powers as regards conjuring it all up, but being a humble man he shrugged his shoulders and said that he had not physically seen what we had, because he had been concentrating on his presentation.

When asked how it came to be that at the exact moment he was describing these things they occurred, Phillip replied: 'They are always with us. They were in my mind and heart as I spoke the words of my forefathers and they manifested themselves so that you could see them.'

It was a powerful message about being in touch with the animal kingdom and what is possible when we are. When we spiritually connect to the natural world magical things can indeed happen. We were an audience that evening not just to storytelling, but to taking part in the grand theatre of nature's unrivalled majesty.

Wild beauty

I have had many wonderful messages from wild animals, and often they bring simple gifts such as a sense of peace, moral strength or a boost to my mood. Sometimes they do much more, appearing as incredible representatives of a divine force – the source of all life. When this happens I know that right in front of my eyes I am seeing an angel in animal form. It's not that an angel has stepped into the animal's body; it is that the animal knows how to perform this role. Don't ask me how, but it happens and I am grateful for that. People who kill, torment or destroy wildlife lose out by not having such miracles happen to them.

It was the first Christmas at home after my mother died, and my sister and I were not looking forward to it. Christmas focusses you on members of your family and when they are not there the loss is especially difficult to bear. Over the years we had fallen into the habit of celebrating on Christmas Eve in the European way, as my mother used to do in her homeland. We would dress up in our best clothes and have a special meal whilst playing seasonal music. On Christmas Day, in the morning, we would open our presents before going for a walk, then back to watch some favourite TV programmes whilst eating home-made cake.

Waking up that Christmas Eve morning, I felt a raw ache inside me. Yes, my mother had been back to see me several times since her passing, but I wanted the physical pleasure of giving her a lovingly selected gift which would make her smile and say, 'Thank you, darling. Happy Christmas!'

Pulling open the curtains, I saw them. By the edge of the white frost-covered lawn, lying down, quite relaxed and chewing, were two roe deer. One was an adult, the other a youngster. Deer sometimes visit our front garden but I had never before seen them in the back part, owing to the thick, wide hedge that runs along the bottom, acting as a barrier to the fields and woods beyond. I had to rub my eyes to make sure that I was not dreaming.

Pulling on some clothes, I went downstairs to take a closer look, for the deer were only about five metres from the house. I wondered what would happen when I went out to fill the birdfeeders and fully expected them to move off, for roe deer are shy and suspicious creatures if you get too close. I often come across them whilst out walking and they always bound off when approached.

My creeping along with a jug of peanuts, some fat balls and a bowl of birdseed did not scare off the deer. They showed absolutely no sign of being bothered, not even staring at me. It was as if we were part of the same family and I was no threat. It was then that I knew what was happening. Of course, the two deer were mother and daughter! It was no coincidence that they had arrived in my garden, seemingly from nowhere, on this Christmas Eve. It was a sign from my mother that she was with us, and understood our longing. Unable to physically return, she had sent messengers from the community of nature. It was a Christmas message with intense meaning, brought not by a commercial card, but by angels of the wild: '*I am always with you. Unseen forces attach us and that link cannot be broken. Remember that we are all part of one family, whether we are human or non-human. Look, feel and listen and you will know it.*'

What astounded me, and still does, is that wild animals were able to respond to a cosmic request to come as comforters. How did they hear this message from my mother, and know where to come and what they had to do? They did, though, and I could only marvel at the magic of it all.

Carefully, I placed some soft apples from the Christmas feast on the lawn and after I had stepped back the deer came to nibble at them, before lying down again in the shade of a variegated bush, the youngster tucking herself close to her mother.

My sister arrived with her husband and, surveying the scene, she simply said, 'Mother is here.'

As it got dark I set the table, lit candles and we sat down to toast absent friends. Suddenly, illuminated by the light from the room, we noticed that the Christmas visitors had drawn closer. In hushed tones, we said, 'Look, they're here.' Two faces peered in the floor-length window. Standing watching us, side by side, were the mother and daughter deer.

The atmosphere in the room was beautiful to say the least, with an overwhelming sense of different dimensions blending, as all life – past, present and future – became as one. After a few minutes of gazing in, the deer moved on into the night and we assumed that they had left for their life in the distant woods. An owl then hooted from the willow tree as we ate our meal and pulled crackers.

Next morning, Christmas Day, they were still there, lying under the same bush. Throwing open the curtains I had expected to miss them, for a feeling of deep connection had already formed between us. Their continued presence was a wonderful sight to wake up to, and the best present my sister and I could have that year. The pair wandered around, coming right past the windows as we breakfasted, and the energy that they brought lit the place up. Life was continuous and these wild creatures were the harbinger of that good news.

Our entertainment that day became watching the deer in the garden as they wandered around, before going back to lie in their favourite spot at the edge of the lawn. I can't describe in mere words how special and memorable it made our days together that year.

The next morning, my sister stood by the window and said her goodbyes to the Christmas visitors. After she had driven off with her husband I went into the kitchen to clear up. It was then that I noticed that the deer had gone too.

Holding out my hands towards the field and the woods, I thanked the deer for spending time with us – a magical gift.

I then sent out a prayer that they should be safe, for life as a wild animal is full of dangers from human predators.

I have never seen them since, but their message lives on in my soul. They had even been happy about photos being taken, and every now and again I look at their images, blowing these special angels kisses, to reach them wherever they now may be.

In the woods

Through a website blog that I write for *PetStreet* I was contacted by Niki Senior about her wildlife encounter. One autumn evening, Niki and her partner, Louis, were on their way to a friend's house, when about eight miles into their car journey something extraordinary occurred. Niki felt her foot lift off the accelerator pedal as if someone else were controlling not just her feet, but the whole of her body. Louis looked at Niki in concern, and asked if she was OK. She confirmed that she was, but then, without knowing why, she proceeded to stop the car by an area of woodland. There she got out of the car and when Louis tried to follow her she told him to stay put, saying that 'something was calling her'.

Niki walked for around two minutes until she saw right in front of her the most majestic-looking deer, whose piercing eyes beamed directly at Niki. As she stood and watched, it seemed to Niki that they were both suspended in time. The deer communicated to Niki that all was not well and that she was feeling bewildered, frightened and helpless. The deer then turned and Niki followed. What had been an intense moment of joy on seeing this wild animal turned into a sense of foreboding. The deer kept looking behind, as if making sure that Niki was close behind. As they walked in close proximity, Niki could feel the deer's imprint of fear wafting around her.

As the woodland grew denser, a fox appeared from the undergrowth and began to approach them. Niki knew that there was something explicit about this, and that it was important for her to keep her communication channels wide open. Following the deer deeper into the trees, now with the fox beside it, she reached a thicket. Both the deer and the fox paused, staring intensely at Niki, as if sizing her up. The fox then stepped closer to Niki and after watching her for a few seconds, retreated into the bushes. Niki took a few more steps when suddenly the fox reappeared about five feet away. With her were three small cubs. As Niki noticed them, the vixen communicated that she had lost one of her cubs and was very concerned not to lose any more. The vixen said that 'the people of the night' had harmed the cub, and she had been helpless to stop it, which caused her great anguish. The fox's maternal instinct was to lovingly protect her young and safely raise them, enjoying teaching them all that she knew.

Niki was stunned at the communication from the fox, but felt blessed to be receiving this information and to be sharing precious moments with these wild animals. However, she still didn't understand why she was there. As if reading Niki's thoughts, both the fox and the deer looked slightly beyond her and down to the ground. Upon letting her gaze follow theirs, Niki saw the most terrible sight. Two gin traps had been set amongst the ferns under some bushes, waiting to mutilate any hapless animals that stepped on them. Horrified and unable to comprehend this barbaric and savage act, Niki snapped them closed with a fallen branch.

It was then that Niki heard Louis calling out to her and looked around to see where he was. When she turned back, the deer, fox and cubs were gone. Louis then asked Niki who the woman was that she had been speaking with, as he could hear a distant female voice along with Niki's own. She didn't know how to answer because she had thought that the deer and the fox were communicating with her via telepathic thought waves.

Animals communicate on a multitude of levels and each of us will pick that up in ways unique to us. The important thing was that deer and the fox spoke and that Niki heard and helped them. They were all acting in the capacity of angels. When the woods, fields and hedgerows are empty, when the last bird has sung its last song – then we will all be doomed and the angel animals will have left us as a lost cause. It's essential to protect wildlife, so we not only enjoy seeing creatures in their natural habitats, but are able to receive their beneficial messages to us.

Everyday messages

There are numerous ways that animals connect to us soul to soul, and not always in grand, dramatic ways either. I teach my students that it is important to get into the habit of looking out for small details, not just to expect some great revelation to come crashing down around their ears, or a luminous orb to appear in front of them. Angels are much more subtle than that.

Imelda lives in Holland where her work involves helping people reach their personal potential through contact with horses. She also teaches this subject and when her apprentices arrive Imelda stresses to them the importance of getting in touch with nature.

She told me that on one particular occasion a white dove appeared and sat in the middle of a footpath, intently watching a bereaved client that she was with. Imelda had a strong feeling develop within her that the dove represented the mother watching over her bereft son, bringing him healing. Of course a sceptic may say it's only a dove, and we are reading too much into it. I think that people who scoff in this way miss much that is of significance.

Another time, when Imelda was telling her students about a heron who had brought her a message, a dog suddenly appeared from nowhere. He trotted into the middle of the group as they stood in a circle, looked at everyone, and then went up to each person, touching them with his nose as if to say, 'It's true!' The dog then walked away, back to wherever he came from.

Yearning to be free

I find circuses with performing animals ghastly, and in *Hands-on Healing for Pets* I wrote about how I once came across a place that used to house abused circus animals and the effect it had on me. I could actually hear the imprint of screaming animals as well as smell their fear. I also detest zoos and wildlife parks, hating to see animals, birds and sea creatures confined in unnaturally small, artificial areas. There are, of course, respectable organisations that are genuinely involved in conservation programmes for endangered species, putting the needs of the animals first rather than treating them as exhibits, as well as responsible places which rescue abused or sick wild animals, providing a stimulating natural environment and rehabilitating where possible.

Several years ago, whilst filming for a programme about the supernatural, I visited a wildlife park. The penguins kept getting infections and a few had died. The staff were mystified as to the cause and wondered if perhaps I could help them.

If I had been a penguin in that place I too would have felt ill. They were housed in a small barren area, which comprised of a dirty pool in front of an artificial rocky pile. Around the front of the pool, where the public passed, was a concrete edging – the only level place for the penguins to lie. Needless to say, many people would lean over and touch the birds, which would then jump into the water to get away. To be honest, I was staggered that no one else was seeing what I could see – namely that the penguins were under extreme stress, resulting in illness.

I made suggestions to the manager that the birds' area be greatly enlarged, with areas that the public could not access so they had a private space, as well as being redesigned so that people could not actually touch them. He told me that would put people off visiting, so the park couldn't make the changes. Couldn't I perform a miracle cure instead?

I yearned for these birds to feel the snow and ice of their homeland under their feet, and to be able to jump into the ocean. All I could do was show them that image, sent from my heart to their hearts. My soul that day was hurting at the conditions that humans often subject animals to.

There was another filming occasion I took part in, in a reptile house. A member of staff asked me to communicate with a snake which would not come out to be viewed as, until it did, it would not make a good exhibit. A glass box was pointed out and I could see a shape under a green mat, which on closer inspection was, ridiculously, imitation grass made of plastic. When I asked questions about the snake's history, I was told that it had only been in captivity for two weeks, before which it was living in a rainforest. It had been captured with many other creatures when the area was cleared by logging. No wonder the snake was hiding. There was nothing positive that I could say to the poor animal, which would never again have any moments of pleasure.

I have never forgotten that snake: one day it was surrounded by the song of tropical birds, monkeys calling, warm rain falling or misty sun filtering through the trees whilst it slithered happily about its business, having a family life and catching food as it wished. Then the next day to be stuffed into a bag and sold thousands of miles away as an exhibit. All animals have feelings. I found the treatment of the snake so gruesome and lacking in humanity that it shook my equilibrium for a long time. So that, and many other such instances, is why I do not support places whose business is confining and exhibiting wild animals.

A few years ago I went on a short holiday. The hotel gardens were beautifully laid out, but it was impossible for me to rest, because all I could see were the rows of cages along one side containing solemn-looking parrots. At around four o'clock each afternoon the birds squawked loudly. It was feeding time and the only diversion in an otherwise boring day.

One pair of birds in particular drew my attention – two Marajo yellow-headed Amazon parrots native to Brazil. Apart from a roosting box, two perches and a rope strung across from one side to another above the stone floor, the cage was bare. Standing before these birds I could hear the female talking to me.

'I yearn for a piece of the bush.'

In front of the cage grew tall twiggy grass. Snapping off a piece of the plant, I poked it through one of the tiny mesh squares, and the parrot hopped down and took it. Then she did something that I was not expecting. Swooping up to the perch from which her mate was watching, she gave the piece of twig to him. The male parrot took it in his beak for a moment before offering it back to the female parrot. It was probably the only joy they had known in a stultifying existence of boredom. They then sat, head to head, holding the greenery between them. I stood and watched them for several minutes as they did this, before walking away with tears in my eyes at the cruel injustice of caging animals and birds.

Wherever I go, I tune into animals and if I can do something for them I will. On that occasion I had been able to fulfil the parrot's wish to give her mate a gift, no doubt something that parrots often do in the wild. It was a crumb of comfort for these birds in their life of imprisonment. I also wrote a letter of complaint to the hotel about the sad cooped-up birds; it was the least I could do. Every good deed that we do registers in our being, and when they read that our pets give us a paws-up for listening.

The natural world can boost animal communication skills.

Scrutinise – Watch nature and its abundant life. Wildlife is even to be found in cities. Look carefully at everything around you, observing the tiniest insect as well as the larger wild animals. Take on board details such as shape, colours, texture, and what the animal is doing. This will help you to become more observant with your own pets.

Absorb – Allow yourself to connect to the world that the creature you are watching inhabits. What must it feel like to be that creature? This will help you to tune into other life forms and keep you grounded.

Research – Look up information about the things that you see to build up your knowledge. This will help you to understand your relationships with other beings.

Help – Where you can, become involved with helping and conserving nature. This will help to develop your sensitivity to animals, an essential quality needed for communicating with pets.

Happiness – Is found in simple things and there is plenty of that to be experienced in nature. Pets like being in nature as it is a familiar territory for them, so it's a good place to share.

We are all connected

There is a part of all life in every cell, and in every being, so in essence we are connected to everything. Nature in its complete form represents our spirituality and who we are. That is why it is so important to allow nature to inspire us and stir the soul. You never know when a wild angel will connect to the light that radiates from within you. Watch for 'coincidences' as animal angels respond to your openness to know more about them.

Nature is a world full of angelic voices.

7 Angel Pets at Work

When pets have a job to do,
they know more than we think.

Life can produce knocks and setbacks, leaving us frustrated, angry, unfulfilled, sad or depressed. Then along comes an animal, and we have an outlet for the love that is bottled up inside us, allowing us to pour it out. In taking care of a pet, we have a focus for our caring and nurturing nature. To love and be loved for who we are, warts and all, means that burdens feel lighter.

Pets can have a positive impact on our lives, but with it comes great responsibility. We have an obligation to animals, for it must never be a one-way relationship. Making us smile is a gift that angel pets can bestow, but we also have to make sure that the pet is happy too. If we do not shower a pet with love then eventually they withdraw within themselves, their angel light dimmed. If we love selfishly, depriving a pet of freedom and expression, then he or she will be heartbroken.

We can share with a pet this sentiment:

I love you. Give me your love and I will magnify it, until it becomes the brightest sun in the universe. Then I will pass that back to you, so that you are love personified.

Pets as Therapy

Animals have moral qualities. As well as being important for their own survival, it seems that these attributes extend to their wanting to help us. We can consider pets as angels of mercy through the things they do for us, which can be everyday things such being around us, as well as amazing feats involving the sixth sense.

Specially trained and giving animals are called service pets. In residential care homes, hospices, special needs schools and many other establishments, contact with special dogs and cats brightens many a day. In the UK a leading organisation is *Pets As Therapy* (the animals are known as PAT cats and dogs) and my dear friend Valery Johnson is a trustee of this charity.

Besides assessing other people's pets for their suitability, for many years Valery has trained her own dogs for this work, so she took me along to meet some new recruits, where I learned about what makes a good *Pets As Therapy* dog and cat. First and foremost, there must be trust and partnership between the owner and the pet. The handlers must like people, because if they don't, the animal will pick up on that energy and also become wary of who they meet.

The dogs and cats must be friendly with strangers, relaxed in different environments, not mind noise and be totally reliable in all situations. It's essential too that PAT cats and dogs should not mind being touched and patted by children and adults with all sorts of mannerisms. The pets need to be OK about travelling in vehicles to their places of work. A pet that becomes stressed on the way to an assignment is not going to be able to interact calmly with people once it has arrived. Dogs are chosen for their calm confidence and should make soft eye contact, as well as express joy in their work without being too boisterous. A dog that sits or lies barely moving can be mistakenly thought a good candidate for therapy work, but this is not the case. In such instances the dog is shut down – maybe wary, fearful or nervous. Cats need to be trained to walk on a harness and should not try to hide or defend their space, but be interested in meeting new people, rubbing against them and sitting on laps. Dogs, cats and their handlers should all express a sunny personality in order to be successfully awarded their *Pets As Therapy* status.

Gypsy's powers

Gypsy, a blue merle sheltie, was Valery's most famous PAT dog. She was amazingly intuitive, frequently demonstrating her special powers at the care home where she always did her very best to cheer up the residents. Being elderly, the residents often had to go into hospital for a few days, and while they were gone Gypsy would still go into their rooms and make her observations. When the residents returned Gypsy would greet them like long-lost friends with much tail-wagging and doggy smiling.

One day Gypsy marched straight past the open door of a room without even glancing in. The occupant, a woman whom Gypsy knew well, had gone into hospital but had been expected to return. Even when encouraged to enter the room, Gypsy was totally disinterested in doing so. Valery intuitively knew by Gypsy's manner that the old lady had died, and this turned out to be the case. From then on, if Gypsy walked past the room of someone who was away, you knew that they would not return. We can only marvel at Gypsy's superior intelligence in this respect.

The first time that Gypsy visited an Alzheimer's home she was introduced to a very difficult man who refused to speak, lashing out at everyone instead. An attending doctor had noticed a photo on the man's bedside cabinet of him in his prime, with his arms around a dog. It was a long shot, but the doctor wondered if meeting a dog could help. Gypsy was the perfect choice for this sort of challenge and as soon as he saw her, the man's eyes lit up. Gypsy worked her magic, reaching a deep level of soul-to-soul communication, and the old man started to speak to Gypsy. Eventually he progressed to talking to the staff and needless to say the doctor was delighted, because meeting Gypsy had transformed his patient's life for the better.

Gypsy also went to great lengths to comfort people, such as on the occasion when an old man suffering from Alzheimer's became very agitated. The staff couldn't calm him down, but through her angel powers Gypsy did. She got up onto the man's lap and, not fazed by his thrashing movements and the shouting, soothed him. Between dog and old man flowed a healing communication which brought peace.

Another time Valery heard a bump and, on turning, saw a woman lying on the floor who then became distressed. Gypsy immediately ran over and lay down by the woman, face to face. Snuggling her body into the woman's, Gypsy had an immediate calming effect. The staff at that home became very interested in how Gypsy reacted to various situations and loved to watch her at work. When I met Gypsy she was an old dog, but you could not fail to notice her strong angel spirit.

Saintly Denzil

I talked to Penny who has both a dog and a cat registered with *Pets as Therapy*. Her two-year-old cat, Denzil, intrigued me as I had heard that he is a very popular therapist, who has been a laid-back character right from when he was a kitten. Once a week Penny takes Denzil to a care home where his fantastic nature is a mood enhancer. Denzil has the place mapped out now and knows exactly where he has to go, happily greeting people and sitting with them. He is a clever cat who reads people's energies, and can tell the difference between those who genuinely like cats, and those who say they do, but don't really. In these cases Denzil won't stay on their laps. If residents wave their arms or shout, Denzil is not bothered in the least and angelically sits ignoring this behaviour, with the patience of a saint.

Barney's healing paws

Barney, a Border collie/Yorkshire terrier cross, is a trained PAT dog and goes along to hospices with his owner Hazel, who is a member of the chaplaincy team. As soon as the special coat and harness is put on him, Barney switches from his everyday way of being into his role as a therapy dog, displaying an extrasensory awareness of knowing which person to go to, and how to encourage them.

Coming out of a hospice one day, Barney pulled Hazel towards a group of people, whereupon he put his head and paws onto the knee of a woman in a wheelchair who was crying. Hazel learned from the surrounding family members that the woman's husband had just died. Somehow Barney knew this and responded to her need.

On another occasion, there was a stroke patient whom nobody had been able to help talk again. When Barney entered her room several people sitting round the bed said, 'Hello, here's Barney.' Barney ignored them, going straight to the bedridden woman, whereupon he put a paw onto her arm and whined. Miraculously, the woman then spoke, saying, 'It's OK, Barney!' We can only guess as to what Barney was communicating to the woman, but it certainly was thera-peutic, and from that moment on she built up her speech.

Another patient became troubled and wouldn't comb her hair, wash or generally take an interest in herself. The woman's records mentioned that she had once worked with dogs so Hazel was asked to bring Barney to meet the woman, whereupon she poured her heart out to him. The next day the staff were amazed when the woman had the hairdresser do her hair, and Hazel found her spruced up, sitting in a chair with fresh clothes on. The woman was so taken with Barney during his numerous visits that she requested he attend her funeral. No relatives could be traced and on the appointed day two chaplains and the crematorium staff sang 'All things bright and beautiful, all creatures great and small', whilst Barney sat alongside them, looking at the coffin. What a very special send-off that was.

Comforting angels

My neighbour Len is a retired vicar, and has given me several fascinating stories. Through visiting hospices, Len has encountered many situations where animals have made a big difference to the quality of people's lives. Len was once giving communion at a hospice when a greyhound called Gemma entered the room, lying down in the middle of it. This meant that Len had to carefully step over Gemma as he moved towards the people who were present. Len recalled how Gemma helped to contribute to the atmosphere of tranquillity, and that it was clear to him that the dog was part of the process of healing.

Another time, Len was standing by the bed of a terminally ill patient in a coma. A therapy dog was brought into the room, which then stood by the woman's bed, staring at her intently. Suddenly the woman sat up, stroked the dog, and lay back down again, slipping back into the coma. The amazing power of animals was once more in evidence. I wonder what the dog said to stimulate the senses of a dying person in such a way … it must have been a truly wonderful message.

Cats seem to be particularly intuitive to death – although I see that event as not an ending so much as a shift in consciousness. Len's mother had been an avid cat lover all her life, befriending the many strays in the area where she lived, and her natural affinity to them meant that she was able to handle even the most skittish. Something remarkable happened the day that Len's mother died in a hospice. A few minutes after this took place, a black cat that lived there came into the room and started meowing, but the noise that the cat was making was unusual, as if he was doing or saying something important.

At first Len thought that the cat had a habit of coming into the room, but a nurse who was present said that this was very unusual behaviour as the cat never came to that part of the sprawling building. Knowing this, it seemed to Len that the cat was in tune with what was happening and was marking the significance of the event. Len knows how important funerals are to people, and he sensed that this cat was, in a similar way, paying its respects to a life transcending the physical body.

On another occasion Len recalled how a cancer-stricken woman in her sixties entered a hospice and had her cat to live with her whilst she was there. When the woman died the cat was found curled up on her. Len recalls that the peacefulness of the cat was reflected in the woman's death.

I believe that these cats kept vigil in a way that humans cannot fully understand, and helped those people make the transition to a higher life. Most of us would not wish to die alone, and would of course wish to be accompanied by a comforting angel. For many, that angel presence is a pet.

With their spark of angel compassion,
pets enjoy supporting people.

Incredible dogs

In their guardian angel role, dogs can help transform people's lives from dependence to having independence. Deafness, loss of sight or loss of mobility can be very isolating, and specially trained dogs offer the person involved increased independence, greater confidence, comfort, a feeling of security and, of course, their friendship and devotion. Dogs become people's eyes and ears, and can even move objects or fetch them with their mouths for their owners when asked.

Just having a dog close by also has a therapeutic aspect, apart from any practical help they provide. During the course of writing this book, I contacted several organisations and individuals and asked: 'Do any of your animals display a special sense, an awareness which results in helping, way beyond what they are trained to do?' The stories flooded in, as evidence that pets are indeed working on a deep level of communication with their owners.

Before she got Bertie, a Yorkshire terrier, from Hearing Dogs, Gill had been in the pits of depression, and never went out. In fact, she rarely got up in the mornings and became suicidal – but then Bertie came along, and Gill credits him as her saviour. Bertie demonstrated his sixth sense for all to see the day he saved someone's life. When Gill was in hospital, Bertie alerted the medical staff when another patient's oxygen levels dropped so low that she almost lost consciousness.

Another Yorkshire terrier, Fraser, may be small in stature but has a very big heart. In 2006, Fraser was named 'Heroic Dog of the Year' for alerting Dawn when her child was ill. Amazingly, when he performed his heroic deed Fraser had only been with the family for a few weeks. Dawn explains, 'I was upstairs and my four-year-old daughter Emily had gone to the bathroom. The next thing I knew, Fraser was tapping me on the leg like he does when the doorbell rings. This time though he was tapping me very hard, and in a different way, as if he knew something was wrong. I asked Fraser: "What is it?" and he led me to the top of the stairs, where I saw that Emily had collapsed and was crying.' When the hospital doctors asked Emily what had happened she said that she had a bad pain in her tummy, which made her cry. Fraser came to lick her face, and she knew that he would go and get her mother.

Owing to immune system problems, nun Sister Marika has numerous allergies, including to dog hair. Marika could not believe her eyes when an email arrived from Hearing Dogs to say that they had acquired a Chinese Crested Dog, a hairless breed, from an animal shelter. Called Amos, meaning borne by God (which Sister Marika took to be a good sign), the little dog was very nervous and shy to begin with, as he had had a dreadful start in life. Amos had been unloved and unwanted, and in the early days would often flinch with other people. However, in Marika's care, Amos matured into a happy, fun-loving dog.

Seven months into their partnership, Amos showed what he was capable of in the most remarkable way. One afternoon Marika put the automatic kettle on, but then changed her mind about having a drink. Knowing that the kettle would switch itself off, she went to check her emails before going out shopping. As she sat at the computer, Amos came up and tapped urgently at her knee, before leading her to the kitchen and staring intently at the kettle. It was very hot, having boiled dry because the lid had not been pushed down properly. Had Amos not alerted Marika and she had gone out as planned, the kettle would have caught fire. Amos had intuitively known that the situation was dangerous for Marika, and that he needed to warn her.

Amos's story reminds me of Kate's experience with her clever canine companion. Kate has a congenital condition that from the age of eight caused her to progressively lose both her hearing and her sight. Because of this, Kate has a very special and clever dog called Flo, who was bred and trained by the Guide Dogs for the Blind Association before undergoing further training with Hearing Dogs. Flo is a Labrador golden retriever cross. As well as making people aware of Kate's dual sensory loss, she has developed an important role in the community.

One evening, it became clear that Flo wanted to communicate something important to Kate. At the time, Kate simply thought that Flo wanted to go outside, but the next morning she found out that there had been a burglary two streets away at the precise moment that Flo had become agitated, and that the police had caught the culprit hiding in Kate's shed. A few days later, Flo alerted Kate in the early hours. Again, she learned from the police that at the time that Flo had done this, a nearby house had been broken into. The police were so impressed by Flo that they told Kate to call them if Flo alerted her again in the night. There are many comings and goings in the area, but through her extraordinary sensory powers, Flo knows the difference between right and wrong.

Kenny's friend Troy is another example of the wisdom of animals. Kenny was in the army for thirteen years and lost most of his hearing through the noise of guns, grenades and heavy machinery. Then one day he had a bad accident resulting in brain damage, which led to his experiencing mood swings. And, if that was not bad enough, he had a stress-induced heart attack. Everything changed overnight and Kenny never worked again. Poignantly, he said: 'My life was gone.'

Along came hearing dog, Jack Russell terrier Troy. Kenny says of him: 'He is my life now, my mate, everything you could ask for. He is me.'

The pair were out walking one day when a car drove up alongside them; it was about to turn into a driveway, but

Kenny didn't hear it. Troy, however, stopped Kenny from stepping in front of the car, saving him from harm. What I find really fascinating is that Troy understood what the repercussions would be if he did not warn Kenny about the car, showing an ability to understand cause and effect.

The organisation Canine Partners is determined to make life better for people with physical disabilities, most of whom use wheelchairs. Every partnership between dog and human is special in its own unique way because the people involved have a variety of different conditions, some of which have been experienced since birth and others that have been acquired during the course of their lifetime.

Eli, a Labrador retriever cross, is the canine partner of thirty-year-old Lorna, who suffers from cerebral palsy. Every time that Eli does something for Lorna, Lorna feels as though she is actually doing it for herself, such is the blending of their energies. After waking Lorna in the morning, Eli goes to fetch his collar and special coat, opens and closes the bin after breakfast, puts his food bowl in the sink and puts the mobile phone on Lorna's lap. He also opens drawers so that Lorna can take things out, passes her the TV remote control, takes her shoes and socks off, and helps her to remove her coat. At bedtime Eli pulls the duvet over the top of Lorna, gives her a hug and then goes to his own bed.

For a dog Eli is incredibly tidy, and will pick up anything that Lorna drops, as well as everything that is lying around if it is not in the right place, particularly shoes. One day a pencil was lying on the floor and, noticing it, Eli picked it up and placed it by the phone. Not satisfied with his housekeeping, Eli then staightened the pencil with his nose! Lorna couldn't believe what she was seeing and says that Eli was very chuffed with himself afterwards.

Although she was only twenty-four years old, Tony became housebound when she was struck down with severe epilepsy. As she felt useless and completely dependent on her husband, Dan, her situation was at first very hard for Tony to take. Her falls during seizure attacks had resulted in many injuries and broken bones, but when Tony commenced training with her first support dog, Border collie Rupert, her life began to improve.

Rupert had been saved from a life of abuse and neglect but once he had been nursed back to health with lots of TLC, he became a confident and assertive dog who took control of situations. On one occasion, when Tony had a seizure, Rupert let himself out of her bedroom, then opened the front door and the garden gate, and alerted Dan, who was chatting to the milkman. Dan at first didn't catch on, thinking that he had left the door and gate open himself, so he returned Rupert to the house. Resuming his conversation, Dan was surprised when Rupert reappeared and tugged at his sleeve, as if to say: 'Come on, pay attention!' This time Dan got the message and swiftly went to Tony's aid.

Like many dogs that I have come across, Rupert had a wicked sense of humour and could make Tony smile even on her bad days. Rupert had been trained to pull out the bath plug if Tony was bathing and had a seizure. One day Rupert thought that it would be entertaining to open the bathroom door whilst Dan was relaxing in the bath and steal the plug, then sit just out of reach with it in his mouth as the water drained away. A naked and shivering Dan was not amused, however – particularly as this took place in full view of carpet fitters working outside the bathroom!

There are numerous other incredible ways in which dogs become heroes and can be regarded as angels. Some charities improve the quality of life for people with disabilities, including epilepsy and autism, by training dogs to act as safe and efficient assistants. Specially trained dogs also help military veterans who have been injured or traumatised in war zones, healing their emotional scars as well as helping with daily tasks. Dogs are known to sense cancers too. A client told me about his Schnauzer, who would lick a particular place on his father's leg, which was several months later found to have a tumour.

But let's not forget cats! Cats know when we are ill and, lying next to us, can offer their own brand of healing help. Their independent nature means that cats cannot be trained to perform the physical tasks that dogs can, but their role in healing hearts and minds should not be overlooked, and they too can help us out, as many of my stories reveal.

Unofficial angels

It's not just those dogs and cats who have 'official jobs' who can sense when people need comforting. Anne from Wales was born with numerous disabilities, including cerebral palsy and a condition that prevents her swallowing. On her eleventh birthday her parents gave in to her desire to have a dog. In a pen at a local shelter was Bruce, who had been ill treated then dumped. Despite his sadness, Bruce looked at Anne and saw something to believe in. As she stood in front of Bruce, Anne heard him say: 'If you look after me, I will look after you.'

During the journey home Bruce was determined to sit on Anne's lap, despite spilling over in every direction. In her tribute to him, Anne described their relationship to me:

'When Bruce stood on his hind legs, he was as tall as I was. He knew that one of my miseries was not being able to dance, so he taught me, acting as the male partner for everything from Irish dancing to a weird form of ballroom. When I was due to leave Bruce behind for the first time, despite the fact I promised him I would be back at school half term, he waited at the gate for me for three days. When half term came, Bruce greeted me with, "There you are! I've waited for you for so long."

'Later that holiday, Bruce pulled me out of the stream when I fell in. It wasn't that deep, but the fact he was willing to jump in fearlessly and save me when he hated water, was a revelation. As I grew older, he predicted my health problems, twice raising me from episodes of deep unconsciousness when I collapsed, and always ready to listen to any difficulties.

'He was my longest-standing boyfriend, remaining loyal and raising me up from the dirt when men found they lacked the strength to stick around. Bruce always trusted me and when I thanked and praised him he would always answer: "I try to please. Do I please?" to which I would reply, "*Of course.*"

'I held Bruce at the end of his life, when he was aged eighteen, and told him how much I loved him, praying that our connection would survive his transfer into the beyond. And it has, for Bruce still looks after me. I both see and sense him around.'

Issy from Scotland told me about a marvellous golden retriever called Opal, who had healing powers. When Opal was a young dog he could be quite skittish around children, so Issy was a bit apprehensive when a friend's young son with Asperger's syndrome asked if he could walk the dog in the park. Opal stuck to the child, though, never pulling away, and those watching noticed a sense of calmness between them.

One of the animal welfare organisations I am in contact with is in Italy, run by an Englishwoman called Fiona. Her website petsinitaly.com has become the focus for homeless and destitute animals, all attached to sad or shocking stories. One day something happened that Fiona had not bargained for – she fell for one of the dogs herself.

'I saw the picture first, an English setter in a cage looking lost and staring at the camera,' Fiona explained to me. 'Then I read his story and started to cry.'

Damn it, she thought, because she did not want to get emotionally involved with the dogs that she was helping. But there was something about this particular one that tugged at Fiona's heart, which responded by aching for him to enter her life.

The dog's name was Gaspare, an Italian version of Casper, one of the three Magi, and it seemed like a magical omen. Gaspare had been thrown out by a hunter who had decided that the dog was no longer useful and, after months spent living wild, the poor creature was a virtual skeleton. Weak and desperate for something to eat, Gaspare came upon a group of villagers having a picnic. Tail wagging, he approached – hoping to get thrown a scrap of food – whereupon he was beaten and kicked.

A passing member of an animal shelter intervened at some risk to himself, and carried the stricken dog to a nearby veterinary clinic, where it was discovered he had two fractured ribs, two broken teeth and severe nasal bleeding. Her mind made up, Fiona arranged for Gaspare to join her own family of cats and dogs.

Gassie – his new nickname – quickly showed a natural talent for seeing to Fiona's welfare. For instance, if he thinks that she has been at the computer for too long he puts a paw on her knee, encouraging her to take a break.

A pet's way of helping someone may not always be headline-grabbing, and we should never be disappointed when our pets don't perform spectacular feats like those we may have read about. Animals patiently teach us to discover ourselves and that may be an angel pet's role in our own lives. The seemingly ordinary pet with you right now is nevertheless very special. Simply touching or looking at an animal can transform or revitalise someone's life. That they can stimulate us in this way is surely a miracle in itself.

Pets bring colour to people's lives.

8 When Angels Weep

The ache of loss is universal.

The hardest part of a relationship is often when it ends, and that is something which affects pets as well as us. We feel empty because our cuddly angel has gone from our sight and our touch. But we never say goodbye for ever to angels because they are always with us, even if we cannot physically see them. Their light does not go out but shines upon us in a million blessings, helping us realise how precious we are.

We may lose a pet through a change of circumstances or death, but love means we are bound by a bond that cannot be broken – if, of course, we want to stay in touch. Grieving for a pet and the repercussions the loss of a pet can have on a person's wellbeing is a recognised condition. Pets too suffer from the effects of grief. Part of my healing work involves helping pets at the end of their physical life, as well as preparing humans and animals who face the loss of a best friend.

From a personal perspective, I know only too well the terrible shock and wrench of losing a pet. When we part with a pet we often hit a wall of grief. Grief is a natural reaction to the absence of someone who caused us to feel comfort and happiness. That 'someone' is often a pet and we feel bereft that the 'person' who understood us like no one else has gone from our lives. How we feel has a knock-on effect with any other pets we may have – as it did in this case, when I was asked to visit a troubled dog and uncovered a very interesting cause ...

Vespa comes into her own

Chris Day, holistic vet of the Alternative Veterinary Medicine Centre in southern England, recommended me to a woman called Susie who was concerned about her West Highland terrier, Vespa. Two-year-old Vespa had lived with Susie's family since she had been three months old, and was described as being a sunny-tempered dog, smiley and full of fun. She was also a dog without aggression, generally uncomplicated, and in good health. At the time of her arrival in the family they had an eleven-year-old Yorkshire terrier called Buzzy, who was the apple of Susie's eye.

Vespa lit up the household with her huge personality, yet she was happy to defer to Buzzy, loving him from the moment she first set eyes on him. Buzzy became weaker as he aged and, being so tiny, had to be carried on walks while Vespa trotted alongside. When Buzzy was thirteen years old, Susie had a phone call as she and her husband were returning from holiday, to say that the Buzzy had been rushed to the vet. Buzzy died two hours before Susie made it back home. It was a heartbreaking situation and Susie described how the family had gone into shock. Although Buzzy had been a little dog, he had filled the home with his large presence.

'Poor Vespa has changed altogether,' Susie said in her email to me. 'Half the time she is herself, and then suddenly she will lie silently with her head on her paws. In fact, now she rarely barks in a cheeky way like she used to. The death of Buzzy seems to have aged her and she seems unsure of how to react to various situations.' I learned also that Vespa had become reluctant to eat. It appeared that her enthusiasm for life generally had gone.

Susie continued: 'The most extraordinary part is that Vespa will now go into a sort of panic, often whining whilst in that state, and dash off to burrow and scratch, usually into the back of the sofa, the back of the car or behind a duvet. She will then vomit up her last meal – even if she has eaten it hours before.'

Nothing in particular seemed to set this activity off; it appeared to be completely random behaviour. Strangely, afterwards Vespa was always calm and normal. She had sometimes indulged in this behaviour when Buzzy was alive, but since his death she had done it nearly every day. The message to me ended with a note that Susie's holistic vet thought that I might be able to help Vespa.

I was intrigued – on the surface it looked like a case of a grieving dog, but it was important to hear Vespa's take on the problem, and as soon as possible. Vespa greeted me with lots of yapping, running backwards and forwards into the house. As I walked in, like most dogs she examined my jeans for smells and information. There was a big comfy sofa in the corner of the kitchen and, as I settled myself down on it, Vespa jumped up to join me. She fussed around for a couple of minutes before draping herself across a cushion, whilst Susie sat the other side of her. Taking notes about the relationship Vespa had had with Buzzy, I learned that tiny as he was, he had without a doubt been the boss.

Size in the animal kingdom often bears no relationship to who rules the roost. I remember once watching incredulously as an eight-week-old Chihuahua puppy – and you can imagine how small that is – ran along a row of horses, which duly stepped back to let him pass. This feisty character then leapt into the bed of a Doberman dog and started to nibble at his bone. 'Grrrr, you get off my bone, you young upstart,' warned the Doberman. 'Grrrr yourself, I'm not doing any such thing,' snapped back the puppy. With a surprised look on his face the big dog stared as the minuscule pup tried to pull the bone away – doomed to failure anyway because it was three times as big as him. With a resigned sigh the Doberman glanced our way, grumbling, 'Stop this raid, someone please. He's stealing my bone!'

Cats too can dominate a larger animal. There was a time when I was watching a family of foxes in my garden who had been having a hard time due to their nearby woodland home being decimated by building work. That night, as I looked through the kitchen window, I noticed that the vixen was carrying some food for her cubs, when a neighbour's cat crept under the fence and started to stroll down the path towards her. I had heard all the terrible stories about foxes killing cats and, with a gasp, wondered what would happen next. The vixen stopped in her tracks to eyeball the cat, which fluffed itself up, hissed and smacked the fox sharply across the nose. Startled, the fox stepped back and watched as the cat snacked on the dropped morsels. When, after a couple of minutes, the vixen gingerly took a step forward, the cat reminded her of her subordinate position with a bare-fanged hiss. Only when the cat had finished eating was the fox allowed to creep forward to the food. The cat then sat a few feet away, nonchalantly washing her paws.

I could fully understand, therefore, that Buzzy had been top dog. Stroking Vespa's soft gleaming white fur, I picked up a physical sensation from her tummy area. Simultaneously Susie said, 'I feel butterflies here,' pointing to her own abdomen. I explained that this was the solar plexus, the seat of emotional energy within the body. It's quite common for people to describe having a feeling there like the fluttering of a butterfly. As soon as Susie mentioned this disturbance, I knew that here was a shared energy situation, with the woman and dog mirroring each other's feelings.

Asking Vespa about Buzzy's death at first drew a blank, and I felt she was closed down about it to protect herself. Upon communicating that it was better all round if she could let go of her troubles, and that hopefully I could help her do this, Vespa turned around on her cushion to face me. She was paying attention to my offer.

'Are we going to go for this, Vespa?'

Briefly, sad eyes flicked up at me before being lowered again. There was obviously something else that I needed to know.

'I can sense that this is a complicated situation, Vespa,' I continued, 'but I need to start somewhere. You are dog, and as such have special powers, so can you be the catalyst that unravels the ball of knotted string?'

In reply Vespa's left front leg languidly stretched forward, briefly touching my thigh.

Then I got what the real problem was.

Vespa loved the people in her life – that was clear; however, she was being swamped with their thoughts and emotions. She was an intelligent, sensitive dog and, in her confusion, she was trying to make sense of the energy that she shared with the humans by manipulating them into positive behaviour towards her. It was the only way that she could cope. Inside Vespa a small voice was whispering, '*Hello, it's me. See me. Love me. Know me.*' Vespa was miffed that everyone was thinking about Buzzy, what a great dog he was, and how much they missed him. How could she compete with that sort of worship?

Owing to the fact that she was still in shock and grieving over the loss of Buzzy, Susie's mind was full of memories about him. When she was with Vespa it was not her that Susie connected to, but Buzzy. She compared one dog with another, and saw in her mind's eye all the things that Buzzy used to do. Susie desperately wanted him back. So, as I always do with my clients, I invited Susie to place her hand onto her pet so that she too could take whatever healing she needed, whilst I worked on Vespa.

Discussing the dilemma with Susie, I learned that she took Vespa most places with her, even to her bed. It may have been comforting for Susie but in this case it was generating overwhelming energy for her dog to cope with. All of us process hundreds of thousands of bits of information every day, and when we are in stressful situations and overloaded we may say 'it's doing my head in'. Vespa felt the same way. As Susie and I talked I was simultaneously passing information on to Vespa, and also listening to feedback from her. It's always interesting having these three-way conversations, but you can't become distracted or else you easily lose the thread.

Vespa had learnt to set up a series of reactions to Susie's thoughts. The dog then astutely assessed and measured her owner's responses to what she did, in order to manipulate Susie away from her mental chaos. Vespa had realised that if she did *this*, Susie would pay her attention, and if she did *that*, Susie would stop thinking about Buzzy for a while. I noted the speed at which this would take place, like a fast interactive videogame, information flitting backwards and forwards between dog and human. Only the dog, though, was aware of what was going on. Also, Vespa's seemingly bizarre behaviour of running around to bury her head was a ruse to get attention. Having tried it once, and got the reaction she needed, Vespa repeated it whenever she felt she needed to.

In her grief, Susie felt guilty about leaving Vespa when she went out socially or for business trips, even though someone was always in the house. Susie would fill her being with guilt energy whilst she prepared to leave home, and then, as she left, she would say, 'Oh, I am so sorry to leave you, Vespa' thereby stoking her regret to its maximum force. This intensity worried the little dog immensely, so naturally she played up about that too.

My advice to Susie was to try several things. First and most importantly, she had to be aware of her thoughts and every twenty minutes or so to think about something that made her very happy (not about Buzzy, though!). She was also to say nice things to Vespa frequently, such as telling her what a beautiful angel pet she was. Then the needy relationship had to be modified so that Vespa could get away from the energy of humans and be a dog on her own terms. I suggested that for a while at least Vespa should be given a choice of where to sleep, so that if she wanted her own space, she could have it. When Susie went out, she was to tell Vespa, in a positive way, where she was going and when she would return. Finally, when she was away, instead of thinking, 'Oh, dear I hope she's alright', Susie was to send out the thought, 'I'm OK and having a great time – see you soon and have fun yourself!'

Driving home, I pondered on the complicated case and wondered how it would go, hoping that Vespa could come out of Buzzy's shadow. I was encouraged, though, by Susie's determination to make changes.

An email came three days later: 'Vespa is a new girl! After your visit she slept all evening and a lot the next day. She was keen to go on her walk, which was unusual, and hardly minded at all when we left her to go out for dinner. When we put her bed down right beside mine, Vespa got in with her toy and slept most of the night. It's amazing.'

As Susie had drifted off to sleep she thought that she saw Buzzy sitting behind Vespa, as though looking after her. Had she imagined it, she wondered, because she wanted it so badly? I am sure that Buzzy was with them, encouraging Vespa to relax. The email ended with: 'Thank you a million times for helping Vespa and me; we are so much better and in tune with each other.'

On revisiting I was delighted to notice immediately a big change in both Susie and Vespa. Their demeanour was more confident, and the cloud around Susie gone. Vespa even gave me the cutest doggy grin as I entered the house, a facial expression of joy. Susie's family had visited that weekend and commented that Vespa seemed a different dog from the troubled soul she had become after Buzzy died. She was like her old self again or, as Susie put it: 'It's like she had an overnight personality change. The weight has fallen from her shoulders.'

As I waved goodbye, Susie had the last word: 'It's so nice to have my dog back. Thank you.' It was good to hear – being able to help people and their pets is why I enjoy my work so much.

Animals grieving

Grief can affect a pet's behaviour or health, which is something that should not be overlooked. After experiencing a loss, a pet will miss having that being – be it animal or human – around. It is well documented that elephants shed tears and I have seen this in horses too. I have also heard that, when a dolphin passes away, the rest of the group swim around it, making loud whistles. With the death of a dolphin calf, the grief of the mother is intense, and she will swim around supporting it for hours, as she tries to revive her baby.

Scientists have now captured on video evidence of chimpanzees tenderly caring for a dying relative. After the event the chimps were subdued for about a month, and the people who observed them said that you could cut the atmosphere of grief with a knife. The researchers from Sterling University, Scotland, say that the studies show that chimps have a highly developed awareness of death. The scientists add that their research with chimps (who are closely genetically related to humans) could shed light on the origins of our own attitudes to dying.

From my work, I know that *all* creatures grieve when they lose friends and family, whether they are as big as an elephant or as small as a mouse. My concern for a bereaved animal's feelings is one of the reasons why I personally cannot eat meat or indeed any foods containing animal-derived ingredients.

Some pets express their grieving through vocalisation – crying, whimpering or howling. Others will search for the missing animal or stop eating and playing. All pets have their own way of dealing with grief if given the opportunity to do so. The grandmother of Emma, one of my students, had always dreamed of having a golden retriever and was thrilled when her daughter gave her one, which she called Cindy. As Cindy matured the family thought it would be nice for her to have a litter of puppies, all of whom would stay with family members.

After the mating, weeks passed and Cindy showed no signs of pregnancy, but then all of a sudden she became very ill. The vet said that Cindy was carrying one puppy which may be dead, and sent her home with medication. Things did not improve and an emergency caesarean operation found that Cindy's puppy was in fact alive. Cindy immediately showered her son with loving licks as he snuggled by her side, and everyone was overjoyed. However, tragedy struck twenty-four hours later when the puppy died. It was decided to leave the puppy's body with Cindy overnight rather than quickly take it away, so that she would know he was dead and not stolen from her.

In the morning, having lain motionless by her lifeless puppy, Cindy gently picked him up in her mouth and carried him to the back door, scratching for it to be opened. Cindy carried her puppy to the bottom of the garden, and after walking up and down for a while, chose a place and carefully laid him on the grass. Then Cindy started to dig. She would occasionally stop to sniff her dead puppy's body as if to convince herself that he really was gone from her, before going back to her digging. Finally, Cindy picked up her son for the last time and, stepping down into the grave, laid him to rest.

Next Cindy proceeded to cover the grave by moving the earth back with her nose and paws. When this was done to her satisfaction, Cindy sat down and, raising her head to the sky, howled like a wolf. The family, who were watching from the window, correctly did not interfere with what Cindy was doing, knowing she needed to express her tormented sense of loss. After about an hour of performing this grieving ritual Cindy came back into the house and, sitting in front of Emma's grandmother, wagged her tail and offered her a paw to be held.

The story has a happy ending though, for a year later Cindy gave birth to five healthy puppies. The family kept one that Cindy was especially attached to and they became the best of buddies.

Sadly, sometimes animals cannot release their grief, withdrawing from interaction with people and other animals. The following was such a case.

Bottling things up

Harry, a four-year-old silver tabby British Shorthair cat, was dull and lethargic. When he was examined by my colleague, a veterinary physiotherapist, she suspected a deep emotional blockage owing to a past trauma. What Harry needed besides physiotherapy was some help from me, she decided, as his emotional state was making him unduly tense.

It transpired that two years previously Harry and his brother had been dashing across the road outside their house when, at that precise moment, a car had come along and smashed into Harry's brother, killing him outright. Completely traumatised, Harry had scrabbled back into the house and cowered in a corner, whereupon he was taken for an emergency veterinary check-up, but thankfully no injuries were found.

The vet had prescribed quiet and rest, but Harry had never been the same cat since that horrible day, becoming withdrawn and lacklustre. He moped around, stopped interacting and playing with the other cats in the household, and didn't want cuddles. The saddest thing was that Harry refused to go into the guest bedroom where he used to curl up with his brother, legs wrapped around as they washed each other and then slept.

Several veterinary examinations found nothing physically wrong with Harry, but as time went by he became visibly stiffer when he walked, which was why he was sent to our clinic. It was important to give Harry healing, and this connection enabled me to hear what he had to say. Quickly I sensed Harry's unresolved grief for his brother – a feeling he could not release. Harry had witnessed his brother's death and the shock from that tragic accident was still reverberating through his system.

As always when an animal has emotional baggage, I say, 'It's OK – give that to me, you don't need it any more.' Of course I am not actually taking it on myself, but I have a technique whereby I imagine pulling the grief off like peeling an onion, then liberating it up into the sky until it disappears.

As he arched his body into my healing hands I heard Harry say, 'At last someone has heard me.' After this we shared a long conversation that I can only describe as taking place in a microcosm in the bubble of the universe. It was as much about what Harry could give me as what I could do for him. I call it the healing dance, a liberating state that we can enter when connected to angels.

The next day Harry's owner was stunned when he greeted her, lively and bright-eyed. Harry then made a beeline for the guest bedroom, going into it for the first time in two years. Edging forward, Harry had a good look round, including sniffing the place where he used to sleep with his brother. After that Harry made a '*chirrup*' noise as if to say, 'I'm OK now', before running off downstairs to interact with the other cats.

Maggie told me of a similar situation. Nothing could be done to save Sam, Maggie's elderly oriental cat, after he unexpectedly became ill. A few weeks later Maggie was sitting with her other cat, Blue, when she suddenly experienced a feeling of immeasurable sadness, which welled up inside her. The sensation grew until it became almost physically overwhelming. Turning to look at Blue, Maggie noticed him returning her gaze, almost trance-like. She then knew without a doubt that this emotion was being experienced by Blue, who had communicated it to Maggie. This sad little cat was desperately trying to cope with the loss of his friend, and was letting Maggie know that he would like some support in his grief.

Many times, I have been with animals at their time of death, not just with my own pets but as a service for clients. On these occasions, I give healing and communicate not just with the animal about to leave, but with any others in the household. Cara, an elderly black Labrador, had a tumour on her liver and, following on from that, a large mass was detected on her spleen. Mary, Cara's owner, was warned that her dog could suddenly deteriorate and that very night she did go downhill, so next morning a vet was booked to come to the house.

When I first received the call asking me to help Cara and her lifelong companion Tiggy, a Lakeland terrier cross, I had another appointment listed in my diary, but after some juggling around I managed to free up the day because I believe that it's important to give a departing pet a good send-off if we can. I arrived half an hour before the vet, so was able to prepare Cara with healing energy for her journey to the next life. She wasn't in pain but felt dragged down by the disease and communicated that she was ready to go.

Tiggy sat by me and Cara, who had a lot to say in her final goodbyes, including many messages about the good times they had shared. Cara told me how amusing she had found it when Dermot, Mary's husband, measured the length of their walks together. I had no idea what Cara was talking about, but Dermot explained that he liked to know how far he had gone as part of his fitness routine, so used a pedometer to give him this information. Whilst reminiscing about the things that had entertained her, Cara also included Mary mislaying paperwork, especially when she needed it in a hurry. Cara recounted how she would sit back and chuckle to herself as Mary ran around fretting.

As the clock ticked and the vet's arrival became imminent, the spirits of animals filled the room. One of them was Frosty, the family's horse who I had been with when he left for heaven the year before. Small rooms can contain a host of angels and that day dozens surrounded us. As well as Frosty, there were angel cats, dogs, rabbits, squirrels, a lion and a gazelle. All elected at that moment in time to help a kindred spirit join them.

When the vet and her nurse came, Tiggy was temporarily removed until Cara's transition to a higher life had been completed. Tiggy was let back into the room to see Cara's body, but she did something that no one was expecting. Giving Cara a cursory sniff, Tiggy then rushed up to me and onto my lap. Holding her close, I could sense that Tiggy was crying. She had lost her companion of over eleven years and it was hitting her very hard. Tiggy wanted some healing for herself now. She had, after all, sat by me whilst I had done the same thing for Cara. After a while she was absolutely fine.

Like us, pets can bottle things up, and helping them to let

go, through healing and communication, makes a huge difference to how they feel and act.

> *Sometimes we need to hold the paw of an angel and help release their grief.*

A Helping Paw

    When a pet is grieving or sad, as you stroke it imagine a pink laser beam travelling from your heart to its. You should feel a blissful sensation as you do this and the pet will be uplifted by your loving link. This help can be given several times a day until the pet shows signs of feeling better.

    Simply saying *I love you* helps a pet to feel reassured. Love activates powerful healing energy.

Time to say goodbye

Animals have a sense of mortality and can therefore comprehend the concept of death. Sometimes they accept the inevitable; other times they are worried about what is to come.

Adverts had been placed to say that *Animal Roadshow* was going to be in town, and listing the experts that people could bring their pets to, including myself. I remember it was a lovely sunny Saturday afternoon, and I was sitting on a bale of hay watching the fun of a dog-agility competition, when a member of the production team approached me to ask if I could talk to a couple about their dog.

The dog was a thirteen-year-old female Welsh springer spaniel called Lucy. The couple with her were concerned about a recent change in her behaviour, namely that she had developed separation anxiety. Lucy had never previously been bothered about her family going out without her, but in the last few weeks had become very anxious when left alone.

A vet check pronounced Lucy to be in good health, so her problem was labelled 'behavioural'.

'What's troubling you, Lucy?' I asked her.

Before I finished forming the question, Lucy's reply overlapped my words: 'I'm ill and afraid of dying alone.'

I had to think about how I was going to relay this information. We had TV vet Joe Inglis on the show, and I knew he had a kit with him for doing tests. There was an opportunity for me to go to the producers and say, 'Look, there is a story here. A dog has communicated something to me and Joe could run tests to verify my work.'

The last thing I would want for myself, however, would be to be told on camera that a much loved pet was terminally ill. Instead, I told the couple that Lucy was not well, and urged them to return to their vet as a matter of priority.

A letter came about six weeks later. Lucy had been found to be in the early stages of kidney and cardiac failure. She was kept as comfortable and happy as possible, until one night she went into a crisis and a decision had to be made to let her go. The letter ended with: 'It seemed as though she was ready, and looked so peaceful and young when it was over.' Lucy had had her wish, to leave this life surrounded by the family she loved, and who loved her to bits.

Cats also show a need to say farewell to those they love. The husband of a client whose cat I was treating mentioned the recent loss of his mother's cat Jason. When the husband and wife had visited a few days before Jason passed away, he had got out of his bed and followed them into the hallway as they prepared to leave, something he had never done before. The couple could see that he was saying goodbye, but they had no inkling that they would not actually see him again. Jason knew though that his passing was imminent – perhaps an animal spirit angel had been drawing close to prepare him. Jason also understood that the abiding memory of his fond farewell would be a very important memory to the people who loved him.

My friend Alison has been feeding two feral tortoiseshell cats, sisters in their twenties, for several years. The cats always used to creep into the barn to eat before disappearing outside again, avoiding human contact. A while ago Alison turned around to see one of the cats behind her, staring intently, the first time it had made eye contact. Alison was mesmerised by the cat's eyes, which reminded her of bright suns. Having to leave for work, Alison thanked the cat for coming. Instantly, with a wave of communication, Alison heard the cat express her appreciation for all that Alison had done for her over the years. It seemed to Alison as though the message radiated through the cat's spellbinding eyes. Alison then understood that the cat had come to say goodbye, knowing she was dying. The cat's physical life clearly did end shortly afterwards, because she has never been seen since, although her sister still visits daily.

No regrets

'I have no regrets.' Bendicks spoke before I could ask him if there was anything that he wanted to tell me and went on to say that he had been much loved and well cared for.

The dog's voice seemed to come from far away, as though he was talking down a tunnel, which was an interesting experience. He passed information on in clipped 'sound bites' like the sort of thing you'd get in a text message. Animals, like humans, have differing ways of expressing themselves and I am always open to finding out their uniqueness. Bendicks spoke like an old-fashioned gentleman would, saying what was necessary with the minimum of fuss.

Aged fourteen, Bendicks had a lot of reminiscences – pictures appearing of happy long walks, bright sunny days and, yes, lots of games. There was a scene of him sitting on a river bank, a young dog with endless energy, and he was staring at a picnic cloth with food and drink on it. 'I used to steal bits of food when she wasn't looking,' he confessed. As he passed this information on to me, Bendicks looked as though he was dreaming – his pleasurable youthful memories being transmitted to me.

Passing on what Bendicks had said, Katrina laughed. 'Yes, that's very true, he did indeed pinch my snacks! I fish as a hobby, and over the years we have shared hundreds of picnics along river banks.'

It's always important to ask a pet if she or he has anything to pass on to their person. 'Slow down and take more time to do things', was Bendick's message to Katrina. I wondered if it would make sense but when Katrina nodded her head and burst into tears I knew that it did.

Bendicks went on to tell me that Katrina had regrets, explaining that 'I have watched as she has looked over her shoulder and thought *if only*. But she must look to the future … walk ahead.' This new message brought more nodding and tears from Katrina. She did not offer an explanation and I was certainly not going to pry into her private life.

Then I was looking at old photos through the dog's eyes, and when I mentioned this to Katrina she explained that only that weekend she had found a box of family photos at her brother's house, and gone through them. It seems that Bendicks did not miss a thing. Angels never do.

Nor do angels leave us. From beyond the grave, a pet's love can carry us along when the going gets tough. I have had personal experience of this, as well as coming across numerous other people whose lives have been blessed in this same way. Some of these special stories follow.

A pet's memories live for ever within you.

A Place in Our Hearts For Ever

Animals invite us to touch them,
and with this comes the promise
they make, saying,
'I'll be with you always.'

None of us lives on this earth for ever, and pets teach us not to waste time worrying about what might be. Instead, they urge us to enjoy each moment. When a pet passes away they go to an afterlife, of this I am sure. Animals are such a good part of creation – in fact the epitome of goodness – that this surely confirms their place in heaven, and therefore their connection to us remains in the afterlife.

On countless occasions, and with a wide variety of animals, I have felt a surge of soul energy leave a body at the time of physical death. During these times I communicate with the departing soul, wishing it a peaceful journey on its way to join the heavenly angels.

When a pet comes back to say hello

More often than not, when someone tells me their pet has passed away and I ask whether they have felt it with them, the reply is: 'Funny you should say that, it's like an angel is watching over me ....'

Walter was Marion's wonderful friend and first dog, a cross between a cocker spaniel, a poodle and a who-knows-what, and the runt of the litter. Having believed she was not a dog person, once Marion saw the shaggy black puppy with his white chest, she was smitten. The dog became the child that she and her husband couldn't have and many years later, when a baby finally did arrive, Walter loved the child wholeheartedly. By this time Walter had developed quite a few health conditions, including an enlarged heart, but a holistic vet worked wonders for him with homeopathy and acupuncture.

Tragically, Marion was diagnosed with terminal cancer, and after much research into treatments, she went to a Mexican clinic where she was put on a very strict diet. Returning home, the therapy was a nonstop gruelling regime, during which Walter was constantly by Marion's side. Incredibly, Marion astounded the medics, and eight years later she is well and leading a busy life.

After Marion's health improved, Walter died peacefully one evening in her arms and Marion strongly believes that he lived until he knew that she could carry on without him. Nevertheless, it was a devastating loss when Walter went, leaving a huge hole in Marion's life.

Not long after Walter had been buried in the garden, a scruffy blackbird appeared with one white feather sticking out of its chest. It visited the garden for a few days and Marion thought how odd it was that a blackbird should have this marking. Sitting down on the step outside the back door, Marion was surprised by how close the bird came, the white feather mesmerising as it seemed to point directly at her.

Holding out some food, Marion was astounded when the bird ate from her hand. Looking into its eyes, Marion felt a strong soul connection with the bird, but she never saw it again after that day. It was then that Marion knew for sure that the bird was Walter, the prominent white feather a reflection of his markings. Walter had come back to reassure Marion that animals do have an afterlife.

Exactly how the spirit of Walter was able come back as a bird is one of the mysterious secrets to which only angel pets hold the key. I am sure that one day, when we join our pets in the afterlife, all will be revealed.

Signs

For years, customers were greeted at my local garden centre by collie dog Jed, who belonged to Toni, one of the women working there. Jed was such a fixture, pottering amongst the shrubs and plants when not lying by the door, that she was much missed when she died aged thirteen.

Toni was sad of course to lose Jed, but philosophical about the fact that the dog had had a long life, and it was her time to go. However, since then there have been several incidents in which Jed has returned from the afterlife. Driving her car a few days after Jed died, Toni looked in the rear-view mirror, missing the sight of her dog sitting on the back seat. Simultaneously Toni noticed, in exact alignment where Jed's head would have been, a feather stuck in the wiper of the rear windscreen. Toni didn't have to think about it. She just knew that it was a sign from Jed to say that she was still travelling with her.

Over the next few days feathers kept appearing; Toni might be bending down to do something and a feather would fly past her and fall at her feet. Other times she would notice a feather when she picked something up or put something down. The feathers appeared with such frequency – something that had never happened before – that on each occasion Toni did not doubt that they were signs from Jed.

Jed also found another way of leaving her calling card. Walking across the conservatory a few weeks after Jed had departed, Toni saw one of the dog's biscuits lying in front of her. It made Toni stop in her tracks because all the dog food had long been cleared out of the house. Jed was saying: '*It's me again, come to say hello.*'

Burl from Texas, US received comfort too when he most needed it. He remembers standing watching his wife feeding their six dogs when he suddenly became inexplicably tearful. A message came to Burl that Flint, their golden retriever, had started the process of dying, but that the vet would not find anything wrong with him. Burl's wife was very surprised to hear this prediction because Flint was in good shape. She arranged for a check-up and the vet did indeed give Flint a clean bill of health. For the next eighteen months Flint seemed fine, with only Burl being able to detect subtle changes in the dog. There came a time when others too noticed a weakness, and a specialist surgeon found that pancreatic cancer had spread far inside the dog's body and that he could not be saved.

The next morning Burl and his wife heard a commotion outside their house, their dogs barking at the cause ... which turned out to be two eight-week-old white puppies playing in the back yard. It transpired that the puppies had escaped from a neighbour's property about half a mile away, and after wandering through the forest, had ended up in Burl's yard. Burl believes that it was a sign from Flint. In an incredible way Flint sent the puppies to console Burl and his wife, with the message 'everything is all right, no need to worry'.

I had an amazing sign of my own a few years ago, whilst sitting in my garden with Teddy and Lilly, who were kittens at the time. Putting my drink down onto the lawn, I noticed a cat collar name-disc on the grass next to it. The hairs stood up on the back of my neck, because it had belonged to Casey. Yet he had passed away nearly ten years earlier when I was living in a different house. Not only that, but the disc had been lost in the woodland behind that house. However, here it was on my lawn – and in pristine condition. How did it arrive in my garden that day? It was one of the many miracles that pets seem to be able to activate, and which I have come to accept as normal.

Sadie, a large tabby cat, used to live with Theresa in Pretoria, South Africa. Theresa often senses Sadie's spirit presence, as it seems does her remaining cat Maxine. When they go to bed Maxine will often stare in front of her, in exactly the same way she used to look at Sadie. When Theresa says out loud that the two of them must settle down together, Maxine lies down as though curling around another cat.

During an interview about my work for a bestselling women's magazine, the journalist Pam got talking about an experience of her own. Her blue Birman cat, Mario, had developed degenerative kidney disease. As time went by and things deteriorated Pam became concerned about making the right decision for Mario so that he would not suffer. However, Pam didn't feel that she had the courage to make the decision – it's always hard to tell whether you are doing the right thing. So Pam asked her angels for a sign. Two days later she went downstairs and there, in the middle of the living-room floor, was Mario's sparkly bling collar, lying neatly in a circle. Mario had worn it for the best part of two years. *That's the sign*, thought Pam, *that I need*. Mario had discarded his collar as if to say, 'Actually I won't be needing this any more.' Pam said that what happened that day was one of the most profound spiritual experiences of her life.

When she took Mario to the vet for him to be put to sleep, it felt absolutely the right time and was a wonderfully peaceful event.

A vision of Monty

Thirteen-year-old Monty went into a rapid decline after he developed a serious virus. Born under the star sign of Gemini, Monty had always been a lively and mischievous cat, and his owners Susan and her husband, Matt, had often joked that he was double trouble. Now, they were heartbroken to see him fall so ill. When the vet confirmed that there was nothing they could do to help Monty recover, they took the difficult decision to have him put to sleep.

Ironically, Monty died almost a year to the day after his much loved sister Bella had. In fact, in the days before Monty became seriously ill there was a strange sense that Bella was around.

The night after Monty passed away, just as Susan and Matt were falling asleep, Matt suddenly had a startling vision of Monty looking young and healthy, his tabby markings glowing as he prowled through the undergrowth. Mumbling in his sleep, Matt told Susan what he was seeing so she asked her husband to send Monty her love.

As soon as she said the words, Matt laughed. He saw Monty roll playfully over onto his side like a kitten, before bouncing up to carry on with his hunting. The vision was comforting to both Susan and Matt, who love to think that Monty is now free to roam wherever he pleases, now that he has said his goodbyes.

Twist's warning

Sometimes people express their disappointment to me, saying that they feel and see nothing to convince them that a pet afterlife exists. When I discuss this with them it is often because they have a fixed idea about what should happen. In the same way as when the animal was alive, we need to be open to the animal's unique way of communicating, and not try to manipulate it. Often, it is when we least expect it that we will notice signs and symbols, or sense a presence. When we accept what is happening without questioning it, then we allow more such experiences to filter through to us. Angel pets are always waiting to fly to us with messages of hope.

Sometimes a communication comes from a pet in the afterlife to tip us off about something. Yvonne used to have a dog called Twist, which her goddaughter's little girl Ellie was very attached to. Since Twist's death there have been several occasions when the child has said that she can see the dog and has passed on messages from him.

Three weeks before Yvonne and her husband Roger were due to go on a much needed break to the Isle of Wight, Ellie said, 'Twist says don't go away.' Yvonne and Roger didn't know what on earth Ellie meant, so ignored what she said as childish nonsense. They soon found out how wrong they were to dismiss this advice. Thirty-six hours into their holiday there was a flood in Yvonne and Roger's home, meaning that they had to return urgently. Not only did little Ellie pick up Twist's warning, it seems that from where he is now, he can see into the future – a sure sign of an angel.

The bond between human and animal
goes beyond death, with pets coming back
as angels to watch over us.

Overcoming space and time

It happens on occasion that while I am with someone's pet the conversation that I am having with the pet leads to a connection with the spirit of a deceased person.

Thomas, a tabby, was an old cat, nearing twenty at the time that I started to give him healing, but he had a strong urge to live as long as possible. Thomas loves his family and is much indulged by them, his every whim pandered to. And quite right too, for he is a ray of sunshine whenever he strides into the room. I particularly like visiting the house where he lives because it overlooks a wide sweeping valley, and every now and again I can glance up and look far into the distance whilst I am working. That seems symbolic to me ... that connecting with animals allows us to see infinity.

I was listening to what Thomas had to say about how he was feeling, as he reposed on one of his favourite chairs, which was covered with a soft, cat-inviting blanket. Over on a side table covered in family memorabilia, I noticed a brightly coloured metal badge. Seeing me glance at it, Thomas's owner mentioned that it had belonged to her late father, a well-known public figure. We talked about him for a while, as I remembered him from my childhood, until Thomas interrupted, saying: 'He's here, you know.'

Nothing surprises me when it comes to what pets say and their ability to accept as natural things that might seem to us to be supernatural. Hoping that the woman would not find it too odd, I mentioned that her father's presence was in the room. Thomas's family are spiritual people and so to them what their cat was conveying was of interest. I sensed that Thomas was a sort of go-between, a translator of information from one dimension to another. There was something note-worthy that needed to be said.

I then heard Thomas add, 'It was not his fault.' I remembered that the man had been killed in an accident, although the details were vague to me. I stared at Thomas as he continued, 'It was an unfortunate set of circumstances that led to the accident that day.'

The woman asked me if there was anything more in the message, so I relayed the question to Thomas. Instantly I saw in my mind's eye a book, although I could not see the title. Thomas was explicit about the next message which I passed on: 'It's a book that your father had and when you open it, the words on the page that catch your eye will explain about existence and the meaning of life.'

I was intrigued: what could this book be and what did it say? I wondered.

The woman told me that just after her father died, she had been given a book belonging to him, which she went to fetch. It was a copy of *Jonathan Livingston Seagull* by Richard Bach. Clasping the book, the woman closed her eyes and concentrated, wanting to be inspired. Looking at the page she chose to open, the woman said: 'It's exactly what we were talking about, quite incredible.'

Several lines on the page jumped out at me, describing how when we have overcome space we are left with where we are at in life. When we overcome time, we only have the present moment. On that basis didn't it seem feasible that all souls, no matter what dimension they existed in, could overcome the boundaries of time and space to visit each other once or twice?

Through Thomas, it had been possible to overcome space and time so that the woman and her father could make a connection once more. Thomas sat watching us for a while, before jumping down from his chair and strolling outside. His owner and I felt humbled by the enormity of being cogs in the wheel of something quite extraordinary – something which Thomas and his animal friends seem to take for granted.

A similar thing happened with a dog called Amber, an elderly, deaf English cocker spaniel who was suffering from cancer. She came to see me with her people, Clive and Veronica. There was a distinct air of sadness in the room when the couple arrived and Clive explained that his mother had recently passed away.

My session with Amber was going well. Just as I was thinking how tranquil it was – with a *whoosh* – I blended with Amber and was inside her psyche. Standing in front of me, just behind Veronica, was a tall woman whom I could see through Amber's eyes. Somehow I knew that this was the spirit of Clive's mother. Clive confirmed that the description I gave did indeed match that of his mother, who I sensed wanted him to know that she was happy in her spiritual home.

It is always of great interest to me when I am privileged to see the world through the eyes, heart and soul of an animal, for the experience shows me how things really are, like looking at a complete jigsaw puzzle. When animals become aware of beings from another dimension they accept this as a natural event, whereas to humans it goes into the realms of paranormal.

Animals experience the sixth sense with absolute clarity and their minds are not clouded by any doubts that force them to become uncertain and to ask, 'Did I imagine that?' Nor do they get bogged down with worrying about 'what will others think if I say that?' Animals are confident in their sixth sense abilities and, equipped with certainty, pay attention to everything they pick up on. This is something that we can learn from our pets – to believe in what we know to be true.

Always by our side

People have often reported to me that they have experienced actual physical sensations when pets have drawn close to them from the afterlife.

Several years ago I went to Monica's wedding, where she raised a few eyebrows by walking down the aisle in a beautiful white dress with her huge German shepherd dog, Benson, by her side. Benson dutifully sat in front of the pews whilst Monica and her bridegroom exchanged their vows. At the reception he busied himself greeting guests and featured in the photos. Later he wandered around the dance floor and I would not have been surprised if he had had a boogie; he was that kind of dog.

After Benson's death, Monica was absolutely bereft. When she visited a medium, she was given a description of a beautiful, loving dog which appeared in spirit form. Seconds before the medium had said this Monica knew that Benson was there, because she could actually smell him. She described it to me as the experience that most dog lovers will know – when they breathe in the scent of their dog, having put their face up close to that of their pet. Benson, it seemed, was happy where he now was, but had drawn close to Monica, knowing she would soon need him for a particular reason.

From that moment on, Monica went about her life as if Benson was actually accompanying her. She started to revisit special places where they used to share walks and, although she got a few odd looks wandering about on her own in wooded areas, Monica knew that the spirit of Benson was by her side.

Less than two weeks later, the eighteen-year-old son of Monica's sister was killed in a car crash. Monica had been especially close to this young man and she told me how throughout the horrendous following weeks she only coped because she felt that Benson was with her every single step of the way. Although he could not physically be with Monica, his spirit was, which was a huge comfort to her, giving her much needed strength at a very upsetting time. I thought back to the time when Benson, a white ribbon around his neck, walked beside Monica, the beautiful bride. Benson still had that place by her side.

Cats that we have had a close relationship with can connect with us in the same way. Rosie communicated with Henry from the day that he climbed onto her lap as a kitten and demanded to be taken home. Sometimes Rosie heard Henry speak in words, but more often their communications took the form of a shared awareness that they both knew what the other meant. Frequently, Henry would look at Rosie with so much knowledge shining from his eyes that she felt humbled – a feeling I often get with animals myself.

When Henry was young, Rosie was terrified of losing him – especially if he had gone out at night. Rosie found, however, that she could mentally ask Henry where he was, then follow that with an instruction to him to come back home. In a short space of time the cat flap would crash open and he would jump on her bed. Sometimes when Rosie asked Henry to come home she sensed that he was peevish about it and he would on those occasions tell her quite firmly that he was busy, or even asleep and not to bother him.

As the years passed Henry's kidneys started to fail, until finally he had a stroke and passed away. Rosie felt steamrollered with grief and filled with an overwhelming sense of loss over her companion. Rosie describes the first day without Henry as like being shrouded in mist, leaving her totally miserable and unable to function properly. Then an amazing thing happened a day later – Rosie had an extraordinary conviction that Henry was coming back to her. She could quite clearly see him with her, and over the next four days this feeling intensified until Rosie was quite sure that Henry's soul was again connected to hers. More than that, Henry was actually lodged *within* her soul. Rosie knew then that she would never lose Henry because, quite simply, he was part of her.

A pet's love is forever

Sometimes messages from animals in the afterlife can come in the guise of a cryptic clue, rather than having a literal meaning. My brave friend Sue loved her rescued donkey, Joan, for many years. When Joan became so ancient that her health failed completely, Sue, being an equine vet, was the angel of mercy who released Joan from her physical struggle to a life eternal.

I had been thinking of them both during that day and, later, after Joan had transitioned to heaven, an image came into my mind of a sunny meadow, covered in mint plants. When I told Sue about this, it was meaningful to her both in terms of accuracy and confirmation that Joan's spirit lived on.

Standing with Joan in her last moments, Sue had wanted to give her something as a treat and, rummaging in her pockets, found a peppermint. Joan munched it happily, sticking her tongue out to savour the flavours.

In a way, Joan's message was spot on, for mint sweets are made from the peppermint oil of the herb. This kind of thing is what makes animal communication so interesting for me, because it shows that we humans have much to comprehend and evaluate.

A Helping Paw

🐾 Communication from a pet in the afterlife can come unexpectedly. If you are struggling to sense a pet, spending time outside in nature can heighten your senses and make it easier for you to make contact. Trying to force a communication can have the reverse effect, actually placing a block on your awareness.

🐾 When the spirit of a pet is close, you may sense this as warmth, a slight movement of air, an awareness that something is near you that you cannot visually see, or you may suddenly have an image of your pet appear in your mind's eye. These precious sensations may be fleeting or may last for a few moments.

🐾 In times of need, we can ask the pet we used to be with to draw close to help us. Even if we do not actually sense the pet, he or she always sends their loving support.

From a pet in heaven

Look for me when birds fly overhead
And breeze blows through your hair

Look for me in the hearts of flowers
Kissed by buzzing bees

Look for me over the hills
And at the bottom of a valley

Look for me in sunlit places
And leaves that fall to earth

Look for me in the morning dew
And nature's love of the day

Look for me in the moonlight
Watched by glittery stars

Love eternally binds us
And I am forever part of your soul

Margrit Coates

10   Talking to Angel Pets

An angel pet's motto is:
'It's good to talk, but even better
when someone listens.'

Within everyone lies the ability to communicate with animals. However, in today's world there are a multitude of distractions that can block our awareness of what pets say. It's when we step back from the hectic pace of life that we are able to tune in and glimpse what a pet is thinking and feeling. Communicating with a pet is not only for an exclusive few – you too can do it. Animal communication is about listening, looking, sensing and feeling. Anything that is approached in this way has the potential to become a miracle.

You are unique and so whatever way or form messages take to come through to you represents your own special way of working: there is no right or wrong way of receiving messages from animals. It's a process of discovery and relationship enhancement between you and your pet. If someone else receives information in a different way or seems to pick up more, do not become disappointed. Go easy on yourself and don't expect too much all at once. Think of it this way: a journey of a thousand miles begins with a single step. Even if you do just one thing to activate communication between the pair of you, this will count for a lot with your pet.

George and his monster

A pet will communicate things from his or her own perspective. This may take some working out, such as the time I was sitting with a young dog called George at a livery yard run by one of my co-ordinators.

'What concerns you about this place?' I asked George, who then conveyed that he had been attacked there by a horrible monster. I was agog to know what had happened, but the dog's owner, Kim, was puzzled and could not shed any light on George's claim, telling me that he had never been attacked by an animal or a person.

'Explain to me what pounced on you, George,' I urged.

'I never saw it,' he replied. 'It jumped out and bit me. Very hard. It hurt a lot.'

This was not very helpful, so I then asked, 'What did the attacker do to you?'

At that, George pointed with his nose to one side of his belly. Kim and I were then able to work out what he meant. Some months earlier George had been messing around the yard when he ran very close to a telegraph pole. As George did this, a large bolt that was sticking out of the pole punctured his side, and the impact was so severe that the bolt sheared off as it ripped the dog's flesh. Hearing George's distressed yelping, and finding him bleeding heavily, Kim had wrapped him in an old towel and rushed him to the vet so the wound could be stitched. George had made a full recovery and the incident had not curbed his zest for having fun. But it now seemed that he was wary of the monster jumping out and grabbing him again.

How interesting that George was convinced an unseen creature had bitten him that day. As a dog, George had no concept of metal bolts and the damage they could do to a body. It was a reminder of how animals can see things in a completely different way to us, and something that we should be aware of when interpreting their messages.

Another world

When we tune into pets we may occasionally actually merge with their consciousness. Vet and bestselling novelist Manda Scott described her experience to me.

'I went to visit friends to clear my head after a particularly ghastly relationship break-up. I was in that no-sleep, blown-apart state where the world feels as if it's made of gossamer and might break at any moment. My friends did what good friends do and told me to go for a walk – and gave me their two working cocker spaniel bitches, who had both just had litters of pups and were desperate to go out. We were five in the end. Me, Inca, Magpie another lurcher, and two cockers, out on heath land which was, by a miracle, entirely empty of other people.

'And then we became a single unit with five extremities. Between one moment and the next, unthinking, I stepped into their world and became a part of this hunting unit. I knew where Inca was on my left and Magpie on my right and the two cockers up ahead. I knew the scent of the bracken and the heather, the grass, stones, rabbit urine, the fox faeces and the bird droppings, and all of it was in such crystal-clear focus that it very nearly shocked me back into my solitude again. But not quite. I've done enough meditation not to grab for the moment or try to hold it, but to surf it, quietly, in awe, understanding that the dogs live like this all the time.

'Inca was beside me, the oldest of the pack, the most experienced. I said something like, "This is where you live!" and she said something along the lines of "What took you so long?" – and that's when I lost the connection. But there was a ten-minute gap in the middle when I knew what it was to be in her world, to know what she knew, to understand the weave of life and death, of hunting and hunted. We didn't catch anything. We didn't even see anything big enough to hunt, for which I am still very grateful. But it changed for ever my thinking of life and death and what it is to be fully present in the world.'

What does it feel like when you step into your pet's realm?

Button and his trust

On the day that Formula 1 racing driver Jenson Button had a bad accident, a Jack Russell puppy was rejected at birth by his mother. Quick intervention by the people present meant that the birth sack was cleaned from the puppy's face, allowing it to take a breath and survive. Both the racing driver and the puppy had had a narrow escape that day, so the owners called the puppy Button, after their car-racing hero.

I had called at a house for a follow-up visit on a dog called Ziggy when I noticed a small, mostly white dog dash into the bedroom as I walked through the doorway. Ziggy belonged to Terry, and her mother Marita was the owner of the mysterious little dog. Marita came to chat as I sat with Ziggy; she wondered if there was anything that I could do for her nervous dog, who was now just under seven years old. His name, she told me, was Button.

Marita held Button on her knee as she sat on a piano stool next to me. He was so anxious that he trembled and shook, and, reaching across to lay my hand onto him, I sent him healing thoughts. Speaking to him heart to heart, I told him that I hoped to help him, and asked him if he had any concerns he would like to get off his chest.

Button told me that he had been abandoned, not just at birth but afterwards. At this stage I knew nothing about the dog's history but when Marita filled me in, everything fell into place. The people who had bred Button couldn't find a home for him and they didn't want to keep him, so he was mostly shut in a stable until Marita had come along and taken him home with her when he was ten weeks old. All in all, Button still felt the emotional after-shock of his first few weeks of life, which he had not been able to release.

After this confession it wasn't many minutes before his trembling stopped, and I sensed that our healing communication was working its magic. Then Button did something that I really was not expecting. He stood up on Marita's lap and reached across to my lap with a paw. As she opened her hands to allow Button freedom to move, the little dog stepped across to me and, without looking at me, made two or three circles before settling down. He lay with his head resting towards my right shoulder, and I wrapped my arms around him.

As this took place I had heard Terry and Marita suck in their breath, and out of the corner of my eye noticed them staring wide-eyed at Button because he was normally terrified of strangers. Afterwards, they told me how they had never seen him approach anyone before in this fashion. I held Button close, not wanting to let this little chap go, for he had suddenly grasped that he could trust me. Perhaps Button had seen me as linked to a comforting angel light, but whatever the reason he came to take as much healing as he could get his paws on. Several days after this incident, Terry contacted me to say that Button's white coat had become gloriously dappled, reflecting his improved sense of wellbeing.

When an animal has such implicit faith in me that I can help them, it is very humbling. These incidents are priceless rewards for my work. However, every human has the ability to dig deep into their consciousness and become a healer communicator. It's a question of wanting to, focussing, and practising. There are many animals like Button that need our help.

Important things to remember in animal communication

❀ Communicate often. You will get better at it with practice, and you will notice more details about your pet's responses over a period of time.

❀ Trust your instincts, which is your sixth sense guiding you.

❀ Talk aloud to pets, giving information about what is going on in your life and how it may affect them.

❀ When you pick up information from your pet, acknowledge it. Say *thank you* when a pet shares his or her thoughts and sends you a message. Take note of how the pet responds to your appreciation.

❀ Try to act on information that you receive and fulfil any requests. Pets become frustrated and feel let down if you ignore them or don't listen. They are trying to help and have important things to say to us.

🐾 Act on your intuition and don't be put off by other people's opinions, or those who are not so in tune with your pet as you are.

🐾 Be open to information coming from any animal or bird source, not just from your pet. When you are out and about, tune into wildlife as wild animals are also accomplished communicators. Being aware of nature raises our consciousness, which in turn enables us to be better able to hear what pets say.

🐾 Our state of mind will influence pets. Studies have shown that negative thoughts can have a destructive effect on organisms. Bitter, vindictive, depressing or anti-social thoughts are a barrier to our picking up information, as pets will naturally try to block negative energy.

🐾 The ability to communicate with animals will be hindered by a frantic lifestyle. Being bombarded by technology shortens our attention span, creating a block to an awareness of our inner voice. We need time in silence and peace to 'be' and not to be 'doing' something all the time.

🐾 Keep the communication channels open so that any time a pet wants to communicate, you can pick up what is being said.

🐾 We need to keep a balance. We are human and cannot constantly live in a pet's world. Animal communication means being aware of other species, keeping a dialogue channel open, delving into a pet's world when required, and always respecting it.

Josie at the vet's

Through our subconscious, we can communicate messages that affect a pet's behaviour. If we do not realise what is going on, this can create confusion.

Josie is a reactive dog in lots of ways; she suffers from numerous allergies and intolerances, including to many foods, supplements, medicines and remedies. She has benefited from regular healing to help with arthritis, but one day when I called she was not her usual self. Normally Josie greets me with vocal noises and much bouncing on the spot when I knock on the door. However, on this occasion I found her lying on her bed, having been sick several times, and having had intermittent bouts of diarrhoea. A phone call had been made to the vet by Isabel, Josie's owner, and a monitoring approach had been suggested, but Isabel had been advised to get back in contact if things did not improve.

I didn't need to ask Josie how she was feeling; you could see how fed up she was from her demeanour. Isabel was obviously worried so I suggested she take Josie to the vet for a diagnosis before it got much later in the day. Because Josie gets worked up when taken to the vet's, and especially during an examination, Isabel asked me if I would accompany them in the car and give healing on the way there.

Isabel's husband drove, and Josie sat in the back between Isabel and myself. Josie became increasingly agitated and I could see why, because Isabel was talking me through all the terrible things that could have befallen her dog, getting herself really worked up in the process. In fact Isabel was so hyped up, her hands were shaking.

It was not healing that I needed to be doing now, it was time for a morale-boosting chat ... with the dog.

'Ignore all that negative stuff, Josie, and listen to me. Let's talk about what's actually happening here.' As soon as I had communicated this with my thoughts, Josie shifted her body and laid her head on my knee. 'That's nice,' I said, before rubbing her ear and continuing with, 'You are a bit under the weather, you are not going to die, but we are taking you to the vet place for a check-up. It's somewhere you've been many times, and after you've seen the vet you'll come home again. You will be fine.'

Josie sighed in relief. Then I proceeded to repeatedly convey the message 'be calm', in an attempt to block out the worries of the dog's owner. A few minutes later we had arrived and Josie trotted up to the veterinary clinic door wagging her tail. The signs were promising.

The vet confirmed that Josie had a gastroenteritis bug, and that the practice had seen many dogs that week with a similar problem. Josie would get over it but a couple of jabs would speed up the recovery process. Isabel was relieved at the diagnosis but then became concerned about Josie's reaction to being injected.

Whilst in the examination room I explained to Josie, in terms that she could understand, what was going on. As the vet stuck a needle into the back of Josie's neck, she did make some protest noises, and I told her that if I have an injection I also say, 'Ouch.' Other than that, Josie was not bothered.

As we walked out of the clinic into the street, Isabel looked at Josie in awe. 'That was amazing,' she said. 'I've never seen her so calm at the vet's before. Usually it takes three people to hold her down!'

I explained the role that I had played by maintaining a supportive inner stillness that Josie could tap into.

When someone is panicking it unsettles an animal, because they are so sensitive to the energy that such behaviour transmits. At the time Isabel was recovering from chronic fatigue syndrome, which locks brain and body into constant heightened stress levels. As Isabel regained her health and her tension disappeared, Josie blossomed too.

Ten ways to tune into your pet

🐾 Spend peaceful time together

Turn off radios, telephones, mobiles, TVs and computers, and get yourself comfortable. Listening to relaxing music might help you release any tension. Or try watching a candle flame. When you are calm it will be easier for you to hear messages from your pet.

Allow yourself to get into a meditation mode, but instead of drifting off, tune into the animal instead of yourself. You can do this by saying the pet's name in your mind. Then ask questions such as, 'What are you thinking?' 'How are you feeling?' 'Is there something I need to know?' or 'Do I need to do anything for you?' Don't force an answer, but allow sensations and images to come naturally to you.

Also try just sitting with your pet without asking any questions, and see if you sense something flowing into you from him or her. If you feel that nothing happens during this session, try another day. On some days pets are more talkative than others, just as we can be.

🐾 Have a clear head

Alcohol, drugs or mind-influencing medication will send out negative chaotic energy to your pet, and he or she will want to avoid talking to you.

🐾 Reinforce the connection

We do this by sending out thoughts of love. Once you've linked through love, remain in the glow that it creates.

Stay in the moment – just *being*, rather than doing anything. Do not have an agenda. Remain neutral when you ask questions, and focus on what the pet is communicating to you.

❀ Breathing

It may help you to relax if you centre on your breathing and focus on it becoming slow and rhythmical. Then focus on your pet's breathing, noticing any sighs or changes in its breathing rate. When you relax your pet should begin to feel more secure and at ease. Notice how your relaxation is reflected in your pet.

❀ Make notes

Have pen and paper with you when you spend peaceful time together. As you relax, jot down what comes to you. You may find yourself writing words or sketching images as they come to you from the animal's mind. Take a moment to work out what the information means.

❀ Keep your eyes open

Animals often make eye contact if they want to say something so keep your eyes open during your peaceful time together. Once relaxed, your pet may stare at you intensely, so that you feel your eyes lock with his or hers. If this happens, allow a soul conversation to begin. It may be only for a few seconds, but the experience will be amazing.

The term 'the eyes are the windows to the soul' makes sense. When we make loving eye contact with a pet, there is an intensification of energy radiating outwards that can be mesmerising. We may even feel a magnetic pull. Through this we can sense who the 'person' inside the animal is. It is not unusual for a pet to wake us from sleeping by staring at us, such is the power of their gaze. However, we should respect an animal's personal space and be aware that staring can be taken as a form of aggression or hostility. A loving look is appropriate with animals who accept our eye contact, but it should not be intrusive. The energy from our thoughts will be transmitted through our eyes; therefore love is a positive emotion to transmit.

❦ Channel healing energy

Healing energy operates on the same wavelength as soul-to-soul communication. Place a hand or a finger gently on your pet, wherever he or she is happy for you to touch. Then imagine beams of light coming out of your fingertips, reaching deeply into your pet's body. You do not need to focus on any specific problems, because healing energy will scan throughout the body and help on whatever level is necessary – mental, emotional or physical.

❦ Sense your centres of energy

Humans and animals have centres of energy activity that receive, process and express information. These centres of energy are called chakras.

– Send a laser beam of light from the top of your head to the top of your pet's head to enhance your mind-to-mind connection.

– Imagine a door opening in your chest as you send out love. It may feel like your heart is extending as you link to the animal.

– As you look at an animal be aware of sensations in your solar plexus. If you are closely linked and your pet is trying to tell you something, then you can get 'gut feelings' about the nature of the message.

❦ Be observant

Notice any unusual behaviour in a pet as well as their movements, and observe your pet's body language. As well as making eye contact, a pet may come and touch you, or lie next to you, as a way of saying 'I have something to tell you'. Sometimes pets point with their nose at an area of their body that is troubling them. They may also turn that place towards you, or even lean it against you.

❦ Listen to your thoughts and emotions

If you suddenly feel emotionally drawn to your pet, it may be because there is something wrong. Thoughts about the animal can keep appearing in your mind. You may receive mental images, feelings, words or flashes of insight, as the animal communicates with you. It can be different each time we connect, and each pet will have its own way of making contact.

Time lapse

Even when we meet animals after a long break, we may be able to carry on communicating with them as though it was yesterday. During a consultation with Terri and Marc about their Dalmatian dog, it transpired that Marc had a special rapport with animals dating back to his childhood. Aged seven, Marc became buddies with two young German shepherd dogs which belonged to a farmer. The two dogs were siblings, brother and sister, yet quite different in character. Whilst the male was aloof, the female was very friendly so Marc became particularly close to her. The boy would spend hours playing with this pal ... arms draped around her neck for hugs, rolling in the dirt, playing rough and tumble games, or sticking his hand into her mouth for her to lick. All tremendous fun.

After a while Marc's parents moved the family away, but he never forgot his special doggy friend. One day when Marc was fourteen years old, he was out walking with his mother when they were confronted by a German shepherd dog. As the angrily barking dog made a move towards them, Marc's mother anxiously said, 'We're in trouble here, let's go back.' At that precise moment another dog entered the scene and, leaping in the air, bowled the first dog over. With a final flourish the second dog swatted the angry dog on the head with a paw. Subdued, it backed away. Then, with eager 'welcome' doggy noises, the saviour dog jumped up at Marc, licking and hugging him. It was his childhood pal.

After all the intervening years, and even though Marc was now tall and walked differently, she knew him. Yet how did she recognise Marc, who had grown from boy into young man? Perhaps he retained the same smell, but I doubt that was the reason she recognised him – after all, she had not been that close by when she sent her attacking brother packing. I believe that this special dog recognised Marc through their soul connection, because once we deeply communicate with an animal that link is never broken.

Years ago at our horse clinic, there were two barn cats, which were both black but unrelated. I developed a particularly close rapport with one, and every time I visited the yard he would appear, so much so that people noticed our connection. We would chat and as I prepared to leave, off the cat would go again. My visits were irregular but the cat always appeared to greet me without fail, whether I was in a stable or out in the paddocks. I could sense him approaching and it was always as if our chats continued where we had left off. One day, after the other cat died, he communicated that he wanted a home of his own. He told me he was done with sleeping in piles of straw now that he was middle-aged. A homeopathic vet visiting the clinic also heard the cat's request. Her cat had passed away and so the vet decided to take him home with her, whereupon he loudly purred in approval. A photo of him proudly lying on his very own sofa now graces the vet's office.

> *When we are in synch with a pet*
> *everything falls into place.*

Individual appeal and sensations to be aware of

Each pet can appeal to different aspects of our personality, which might help us to develop our good traits. Some relationships are slow to develop and become established, whereas with others there might be an instant connection. As our circumstances change, a certain pet may have a valuable role to play in our life. Animals are patient with us, as Rhianna from Alberta, Canada has learnt from her seal point ragdoll cat, Suki.

She explains: 'He has taught me about the subtleties of his nature, voice, and the playfulness of his spirit. Because our bond is so strong he has continued to put up with my poor cat communication skills, but when I do get a message it is very mood altering. The shift is a path to greater communication. However, it often takes me longer than I would wish to figure out that my cat is speaking to me. Suki is a trouper for trying to keep me accountable to myself, and helping me to understand that my thoughts and feelings are worth paying attention to and honouring. I think that he is most concerned as regards the minute details of my self-fulfilment.'

Because we communicate with animals within the realms of energy fields, we may experience strange sensations, which my sister Sue has coined a phrase for. A black-and-white stray tomcat appeared in her garden, where she noticed him taking scraps left out for the birds. The emaciated cat was nervous and refused to be touched, but he started to hang around for the bowls of food that my sister put out for him. This routine went on for some months, until one day the cat appeared with a bleeding eye. Reaching down, my sister expected the cat to run away as usual, but he just sat there and let her pick him up. Sue still remembers the feeling as they made contact, describing a sensation going through her like 'a sort of electric shock with bells on', and simultaneously she heard the plea '*help me*' coming from the cat. My sister did of course help the cat, whom she called Jack, and taking him in gave him a loving home for the rest of his life. Having 'an electric shock with bells on' became a regular occurrence whenever the two of them had a communication connection.

'Voices in the head' and sceptics

Communicating with animals is not the same as hearing 'voices in the head'. People with mental health problems sometimes say that they are driven to do certain things by a voice inside them, urging them on. However, animals do not want us to commit crimes or harm anyone. They do not encourage us to become obsessive or anti-social, nor do they want us to be destructive. Animals through their angel qualities teach us to be spiritual, and what they transmit will relate to things that are of benefit to us, themselves or other animals and people.

There are those who scoff at the idea of humans and

animals communicating with each other mind to mind, and of animals having a spiritual affinity to us. Well, it wasn't so many years ago that animal behaviourists insisted that animals did not have thoughts and feelings, and now they know better. If we allow our sceptical mind to overrule what our heart is saying, we will miss a pet's spiritual ways. When we have an open mind pets can teach us many amazing things.

As I go out and about, whenever I engage someone in conversation and our talk turns to animals, I always ask, 'Does your pet talk to you telepathically?' It is surprisingly common for me to hear that there is a telepathic link between owner and pet. Every day, normal people have deep sixth sense connections with pets, and their personal experiences add to the extensive pool of data.

Worldwide interest in interspecies communication is escalating and will continue to do so until, I believe, it will be commonplace for everyone involved with animals to admit to having soul conversations with them. This, in turn, will lead to more and more angel experiences between us and the pets in our lives.

Mixed messages

We need to be very clear about what we want to communicate to animals. If, for example, we focus on what we don't want a dog to do, we will project an image of it doing just that. The dog, wanting to please, does what it thinks it is being told to do. Consequently, when we tell the dog off, we confuse and upset it. Then it becomes a vicious circle whereby we think we have a problem dog.

Mind images and thoughts are energy instructions. It is therefore helpful to focus on sending an image of what we actually want a dog to do. It may take a while though for us to do this strongly and for the dog to change its habits.

Cats are independently minded and have a different attitude to their relationships with us than dogs do, so I find that this technique isn't so helpful with felines. My cat Teddy likes to dismantle anything he can get his paws and claws into. Beaming images of him lying quietly never changes his behaviour when he is in the full flow of finding out how something is put together. Offering him a titbit does the trick, though, and enables me to salvage what is left of the package, drawer or cupboard.

Naturally, when we take on cats and dogs who have an unknown history, we can be anxious as to how that pet is going to behave. But any fears and uncertainties we have will transfer to a pet. Buster, a young mongrel from a shelter, settled in quickly with Kate and her husband. One aspect of Buster's character worried the couple, however – namely the dog's tendency to growl when people came to the house, even if he knew them.

True to form, Buster growled at me. Eventually, he approached me with a toy and, after sucking it for a few minutes, rolled onto his back. His tummy was irresistible to tickle and now was the time to talk. And this is what Buster told me …. The first time that someone had knocked at the door of his new home he had growled, because he was unsure of what would happen. When Buster did it again with the next visitor a pattern set in. The more that Kate and her husband became anxious and anticipated Buster growling, the more they reinforced this behaviour, through their inadvertent mental instructions.

To resolve this problem, the couple had to stop thinking about Buster growling and to form instead an image in their minds' eye of him happy and relaxed. Most importantly, and the hardest bit, is that the couple had to actually *feel* calm and not allow any tension into their energy state.

After my visit Kate reported a definite shift in Buster. Positive thoughts did help his behaviour, and Kate found this strategy worked even better when such thinking came to her without any effort on her part.

Animals are masters of telepathic communication and the best teachers of it that you will ever find.

A Helping Paw

Touch is a universal language which enables us to receive communication that we cannot get any other way. Practise touching a pet and seeing what comes into your mind the instant that you do this. You might receive a fleeting image, or a sense of something. In what ways does what you feel relate to the pet's life, or your relationship with each other? If the pet is not well, as you touch, send out thoughts of him or her feeling better.

What's going on?

If a pet is acting in a way we find unacceptable we can tune into him or her to work out what is going on. We must always do this by asking questions that will be logical to the animal. It's no good saying, 'You annoy me when you do that – why do you do it?' The pet has a different concept of action and reaction, so we need to approach things in a way that produces information that is helpful to us. Our intention should be to find out what the pet is thinking and feeling so that we can understand why certain things happen in relation to him or her.

Animals receive information from us in several ways. These include words spoken out loud or transmitted in our minds, our body language, our abstract thoughts and emotions as well as our concrete ideas, aims or plans. Animals need to be in tune with the signals from everything around them in order to survive and this is not bred out of pets, no matter how domesticated we think they have become. So they act like their ancestors and their wild cousins, and think that we can read these energies too, which is when so much confusion can arise between us.

Messages from animals may be received by us as words appearing in our minds which offer a clue or describe a situation, like the time when the lost cat Mijbil told Roly not to give up searching for her. Other times we may detect pictures in our mind's eye. These images can represent something happening to the animal, or a situation as seen though the pet's eyes, such as when Snoopy showed me how he was bundled into a car. There are also times when knowledge just seems to appear within us. This is our sixth sense linking with the pet. We may also get sensations within our bodies reflecting what is happening to the pet, including emotional or physical feelings – as occurred when I was communicating with Josie at the vet's and with Harry the grieving tabby cat. You may also sense the flow of thoughts through an animal's mind as it arises, as happened when I communicated with George, the dog who was worried about a monster.

Whenever we pick up on a pet's 'inner voice', that voice will vary from one animal to another, much as our own expressions do. Pets are usually direct in their approach to passing on information because, unlike humans, they have no desire to embellish, distort, or put a spin on it. They tell it how it is. (That is, unless they are natural comedians like my friend Tom, who I mentioned in chapter 1!)

Unfortunately we don't always 'get it' when a pet communicates a message to us. In order to be a competent animal communicator it helps to have an understanding of the inherent species behaviour of the pet we have taken on. This topic is frequently overlooked, even by professionals. The next two chapters share insights in comprehending and empathising with pets on their own terms. Like adding a piece to a jigsaw puzzle, a problem can be solved when we have the right clue.

We should remember that angel pets are not perfect, even though they have magical attributes. Living with us, they rely heavily on our being their ever-attentive guardian angels in turn for the wonder they bring to our lives.

The whole world is full of angels; it's just that pets have never forgotten this. To many humans, it has long been a forgotten secret. The secret's out, though, and the future can be brighter because of it.

Sharing love with a pet
helps us to awaken our soul.

11　Acting Naturally

Looking at a pet's perspective

Sometimes when we share our home with an animal, we may feel that we are living with devil pets, fallen angels, reluctant angels or disturbed angels – as well as angels in disguise. To fully understand pets, we must always be aware that they have thoughts, emotions and feelings according to their own personality and behaviour patterns. It's rewarding to get to know a pet's moods and character, and it's important to accept the pet as an individual – through this interaction we are also learning about ourselves.

Often when a pet is described to me as troublesome, it is actually behaving in a way that seems perfectly normal to it, and which suits its circumstances. What seems reasonable, even instinctive, to an animal can appear unreasonable to us, and the cause of much misunderstanding. Animal behaviour varies according to species, sex, age, breeding, genetics and health. It will also relate to current management and lifestyle and things that have happened – including past handling, training and people's mannerisms, behaviours and emotions.

Bored and frustrated dogs and cats become destructive and depressed – all pets need attention. Too often I have been asked to communicate with pets who have been trashing house décor or their living spaces, and I have needed to point out that the pets are communicating that a drastic lifestyle change is needed for them. Confined pets who do not enjoy their life will have little to say to us other than to express their distress. Pets deserve to be happy.

To get the best out of a relationship with any pet we need to invest our time. Dogs like to please and are keen to do things with us. They are fun to be with when properly trained, and a key to this is that they must be exercised, physically and mentally, every day through being taken for walks.

Through communicating with a pet we can draw back a curtain on his or her world. Light spills onto what the pet has to say, and insight penetrates our being as our two worlds meet. This can have all-round miraculous consequences – often in unexpected ways.

Through her Vizsla dogs, I have known Bryony for many years. Phizz arrived in Bryony's home as a tiny puppy and grew into a beautiful dog. She had a tendency to be reserved, and when Bryony started taking Phizz to dog shows the judges marked her down owing to the young dog's shyness and lack of confidence. Could I help? It was worth a try.

I had a deep conversation with Phizz. About what precisely I cannot actually tell you, because it was more a meeting of souls than a specific conversation. She loved my attention to her thoughts and feelings.

The next day Bryony took Phizz to a competition and she sparkled so much that she won it, getting a lifetime ticket for Crufts into the bargain and later becoming a show champion. A deep bond formed between us that day and, ever since then, Phizz greets me like a long-lost friend when we meet, pushing the other dogs aside to have my undivided attention.

Associations

Things that have happened in a pet's past can cause unpleasant memory triggers. My rescued cat Mitzi had several phobias, which included a fear of people who held anything resembling a stick, of shoes left lying around, and of being shut in a room with the door shut. She was also wary of certain smells.

Humans have far less well-developed senses than pets. As regards the sense of smell, we tend to pick up on one 'lumped together' odour such as coffee brewing, mown grass, freshly baked bread or a particular perfume. However, pets can break these smells down into constituent components and certain smells may trigger unpleasant memories by creating a reference point to their past.

After Mitzi was rescued with her kitten, it was obvious that she had several hang-ups relating to past abuse, including the smell of tobacco. She only had to detect a residue on a visitor's clothes or hands to cause her nose to quiver, and she would bolt out of the room. From what she had communicated to me, I knew that Mitzi's past tormentors had been smokers and to the end of her life she chose to avoid anyone associated with that habit.

Ben learns to love life

I am often asked to help a traumatised animal that has been rescued from shocking circumstances that are likely to affect its mental and emotional behaviour for a long time. Many are cats and dogs that have been the subject of investigations into animal abuse. This was the case with the dog that Connie and Geoffrey brought to me. They were very experienced dog owners, particularly with Lhasa Apsos, so when their old dog had passed away they considered themselves very lucky to find another of this breed at their local dog charity re-homing centre.

However, right from the first moment they set eyes on the

little grey Tibetan mountain dog, things did not bode well. He was withdrawn and very nervous, so much so that he failed to interact with anything or anyone. It was not surprising because the dog had lived all of his four years on a remote farm where puppies were bred without love and care, just for financial reward. Lack of handling, stimulation and socialisation of both puppies and kittens leads to behavioural problems later in life, which is why it is essential to see them before purchase to check they are living in a home with a happy mother.

Used as a stud dog, the Lhasa Apso had been kept in a gloomy shed. Apart from when his food and water were brought in daily, his only other human contact came when the farm's bitches were brought to him for mating. The dogs existed in this way until someone tipped off the authorities about this disgusting place and it was investigated. Conditions were so bad that numerous dogs were taken into care and those that could be saved were sent to a variety of re-homing centres.

Hearing the sad story, Connie and Geoffrey signed the adoption papers to take the little dog home – feeling sure that time would help him to overcome his trauma. The couple also felt that their rural house would be the perfect rehabilitation home for him as, being retired, they would have lots of time to devote to their new pet. Driving home, they pondered over what to call the little dog, and by the time they had arrived had named him Ben.

The rescue centre thought that they had found an ideal home for Ben but he struggled to cope even in his new peaceful surroundings. Because of the breeder's attitude, the dog had missed out on socialisation, particularly as a puppy, which is vital for a dog's overall wellbeing. He had come from a world of near silence and lack of stimulation to a world full of activity, smells, sights and sounds. Ben did not know how to play, and he showed no personality whatsoever. The dog just went through the motions of living but without any apparent enjoyment or interest in people or his surroundings.

Six months went by and Ben remained disturbed by his years of incarceration and lack of care. His new family had a caring vet who prescribed natural remedies, but the dog was such a lost soul that he didn't respond to the degree that had been hoped. It was then, in despair, the couple turned to me, asking if I could do anything to help their little Ben.

I answered honestly – no promises could be made, but I would give some healing to Ben as well listen to what he had to say, including how he felt about himself and life in general. Wasn't that the very least I could do? The couple arrived one fine spring morning, armed with a letter from their lovely vet, which detailed the dog's history and explained that after the six months in which they had attempted to rehabilitate him the dog remained 'troubled and extremely nervous'.

Ben was so anxious that he was a pitiful sight, although looking beyond his demeanour he was actually very cute. He crept in and then cowered in the corner of the room, where he shook uncontrollably, constantly dribbling while I took notes. Connie and Geoffrey wanted to help his emotional state – something that their vet admitted he had no answer for. I was the last resort, but over the years I have learnt not to feel under pressure, because any stressful energy is going to block my communication skills.

As always when going into my 'working mode', I raise my energy to a healing vibration, as this is the same channel for interspecies communication on the unseen level. It is, after all, the wavelength that animals communicate on. Being a healer and interspecies communicator I mix both skills during a session and so it was that, kneeling down, I gently laid my hands onto Ben's shoulder and tuned into his soul. After a few minutes the look in Ben's eyes changed – it softened and the acute apprehension eased. I knew then that our worlds had become one and in that place we could talk to each other as equals.

Looking into those haunted but intelligent eyes, I didn't know to what extent I could help this damaged dog and my heart ached, so badly did I want to make a difference. It was my wish to help Ben find enough stability to enable him to enjoy his life from now onwards. I find that coaxing trauma out of an animal is much like working with a human who has been through a stressful event. But with animals there is the added bonus that you can actually reach the truth of what they really feel, because whereas humans often tend to mask their feelings and thoughts, animals do not. Once we get through the blockages, then in my experience pets are often able to let go and move on. However, each animal is an individual being and what may work in one situation may not in another. I could only pray that I could help Ben, so the first thing I said to him was exactly that.

Ben became relaxed as he responded to my touch, the shaking became less frenetic until it ceased altogether, and his eyelids started to droop. Before he fell fast asleep I needed to talk to him.

'Take me back, Ben, to a time when you were happy,' I communicated wordlessly in a thought transmitted directly from my mind to his.

To hear Ben's answer I 'looked' into the place in my mind where I receive communication from the unseen levels, the psychic link to all that there is. It's like looking at a grey artist's canvas and commonly either images or words appear.

I waited. Nothing came. The area that I was 'looking' at remained a blank space.

I asked the same question again, and after a few more minutes the darkness started to expand into lighter shades as slowly images flashed by me. Ben was thinking. He was going back in time and for me it was like watching the rewind of a videotape – being unable to make full sense of the pictures that sped past me, but getting a bit of the story. Then the flashing stopped and I saw a small puppy cuddling up to several others.

'Is that when you were happy, Ben?' I asked. 'When you were a puppy?'

Sadness filled me in reply. Then the image shifted perspective and panned from the puppies to the mother dog. She was lying on a dirt floor and I could sense her hunger, isolation and depression. The experience was overwhelming as, even at such a young age, the puppies would be able to sense the energy of emotional suffering.

Ben suddenly spoke directly to me as opposed to just linking me with images from his past. His voice was soft but clear: 'I had fun with the other puppies, we played and it was good to have company. That was the best time.'

More images followed his words – of tumbling games, biting ears, chewing limbs, licking faces. A pile of warm bodies with pink tummies, and snuffly, yelping noises as the puppies slept and dreamed. Beyond that, I was aware of an eerie silence rather than a background noise of everyday life and appreciative people. Then I sensed that Ben was alone without his siblings; by now the little dog knew that his mother was very unwell, her health depleted due to her having had too many litters. Ben communicated that he could smell that her death was around the corner, and indeed he told me that he was witness to this occurring.

A man came to put Ben into another shed, where he lived for months alongside other young dogs, all in caged areas. They were selected to continue the obscene breeding programme, and their offspring were sold on the internet, though newspapers or pet shops. Often offered as 'home bred', many of the puppies had health problems owing to inbreeding.

More of his memories followed – they were of an endless cycle of boredom and yearning; of staring up at a small dirty window, straining to make sense of changing patterns on the glass, the distant sounds, cold turning to clammy heat and back again to cold, as Ben spent the next years of his life in isolation – a cruel thing to do to any animal. As the images ceased Ben looked up at me. Was that a personality I could see shining out of those staring eyes?

'Tell me about the time when you left that horrible place, Ben.'

Ben's eyes flickered and simultaneously more of his past emotions swamped me. When the shed door had opened and a group of humans had walked in to save him from further misery, I realised that Ben had gone into shock. There was such a lot to take in – the noise of humans jabbering, mobile phones ringing, his first car journey with its scary motion and the other traumatised dogs in the vehicle; then seeing a world flashing by that he hadn't even known existed. Next came the absolute terror and indignity of being examined in a room that smelled strongly of chemicals. What was that about? he had wondered.

The kaleidoscope of images tumbled on and on, telling me about Ben's subsequent journey to the rescue centre, where someone had placed a collar around his neck, attached a lead and taken him for his first walk. The memories were all there, ready to be picked up by anyone who knew where to look for them, and how to listen to their effects.

From my point of view, I was pleased that Ben was communicating so much to me because letting go is often the first step to recovery. By this time Ben had fallen asleep and Connie and Geoffrey commented that, for the first time since they had known him, the dog's face looked peaceful. It didn't matter to my soul-to-soul communication with him that Ben slept, for the soul does not switch off and now I needed to help him move on to the next stage of recovery. I said a lot to him then, about how deeply ashamed I was to part of a race that could be so inhumane, but that it might help him to know that he was not alone – that the world over not only animals but humans suffer too owing to the dark and selfish side of human nature. I explained that humans have a lot more to learn from animals. Perhaps Ben would find the strength to forgive so that his angel qualities could shine through?

The atmosphere became so peaceful that I could easily have nodded off too, but reluctantly I took a deep breath and, gently sliding my hand off Ben, got up. So much had passed between us – words, images, emotions and thoughts – that it seemed as though we had been communicating for hours. When I looked at the clock I was amazed to find that only half an hour had passed by. Communicating with animals is much less time-consuming than with people because it's mind-to-mind talk, and therefore very direct.

When Ben left with Connie and Geoffrey, he seemed calmer but, with this sort of communication and healing, it's impossible to know how deeply the effects will go until some time has passed. Two days later, I knew just how much had changed when the phone rang and I learned that Ben was a different dog! Apparently, as soon as he had arrived home from being with me, he had been more relaxed. The next morning he had been offered a toy and, instead of backing off and looking scared, he had started to wag his tail as if to say, 'OK, let's play!' Ben then had his first game.

As the days wore on Ben even felt confident enough to be a little cheeky. Everyone was thrilled – not least, of course, Ben. I saw him once more a week after the first visit and a much more confident little chappie sauntered in. During that session he was quite different to talk to, and I sensed an urgency in him to get on with life and make up for lost time. In fact when I asked him if he was troubled by anything that he wanted to discuss that day, he replied, 'I don't need you any more, I'm OK now!'

I laughed – the comment was music to my ears. Job done! I gave Ben a hug before he trotted out of the door, and I noticed a marked *joie de vivre* in his step. Shortly afterwards I had received a thank-you letter from his vet, saying that he could not believe the change in Ben. The vet had done his best for six months but it was getting through to Ben on his wavelength that had triggered a miracle.

Several years have gone by and Ben has gone from strength to strength, his angel qualities shining as he now visits residents in a nursing home, bringing light into their lives through his loving and friendly manner.

I still have a card from Connie, Geoffrey and Ben on my desk. It reads: 'We will never forget how much you helped Ben. Thank you so much.'

Enclosed was a photo of a very happy dog.

What's in a name?

If you take on an animal that has had a difficult past, you may find that your new pet is happier if you give it a change of name, as its old name may be associated in its mind with scolding, deprivation or fear.

Read names from a list to the animal. Then allow your heart to sense which one the animal resonates with. The animal may even suggest a name to you. Ben in the last story didn't have a name when he was taken from a puppy farm. His rescuers called him Bryn at first, but he didn't respond to that name. When Geoffrey and Connie changed his name to Ben, the dog acknowledged them. He liked the name and it suits him too.

> *There is an angel inside every pet*
> *waiting to spread its wings.*

Angel pets make us smile.

Realistic expectations

We need to have realistic expectations when it comes to what animal communication can and cannot achieve. My saying to a dog 'please can you not follow trails, when you do you get lost and this causes your owner a lot of stress' is not going to work; nor would it be any good to say to a cat 'please do not hunt mice as your person doesn't like it when you do'.

I sometimes get calls from people who say 'talk to my dog and say if he doesn't stop barking he will be sent away', or 'tell my cat to stop spraying or it will have to go'. Pet issues which humans find annoying, inappropriate or dangerous need to have their causes unravelled.

There was a cat I once worked with who would frantically scratch her neck until the area was raw. Skin tests had proved negative, and so sedation had been prescribed to stop her scratching. When I communicated with the cat, she told me about a burning pain and tingling in her neck and head, and as I wondered when these symptoms started, the cat said, 'After I was bumped by a car.' The owners could not recollect an accident, although they did remember a couple of days when the cat had been 'off colour' and confirmed that the neck clawing had started shortly afterwards. I suggested a visit to a specialist vet, which resulted in a diagnosis that led to successful treatment. Page 216 has a list of signs to look out for in pets which may indicate that pain or an illness is triggering behavioural problems.

Animal communication means inching ourselves forward from being centre stage, so that we are able to give our undivided attention to the life around us. Only then can a harmonious dialogue begin.

Dangers of a quick fix

People who are not properly qualified in pet behaviour can believe their own propaganda of half-truths, and may not correctly diagnose the underlying problem when it comes to determining the correct treatment for a pet. Advice from someone who advocates quick-fix training methods often results in the relationship between the owner and the animal becoming soured. The original problem may then escalate into something much bigger, but when the bond between pet and human is broken it can take a lot to regain the animal's trust.

It can be tempting to use quick-fix methods, especially as they can sometimes yield results that make a dog trainer look good. The dog, however, can be left feeling bad about the whole experience. Besides leading to the dog losing trust in the owner, such methods may make a dog become aggressive, or exhibit learned helplessness. Learned helplessness means that the dog has 'shut down' and, although it appears to comply with commands and demands, it is actually deeply distressed. If all an owner wants is obedience from a dog then a quick fix can work, especially if the owner doesn't care what the dog thinks of him or her. But if we want friendship and partnership with the animals in our lives, then understanding the individual nature of the animal and the reason for the problem are the way forward.

With dogs, quick-fix approaches include the use of prong collars, citronella collars, electric-shock collars, and collars and harnesses that apply pressure on certain points of the dog's neck or chest. The idea of all of these devices is to deliver pain or shock to dogs, leading to fear or anxiety on the part of the animal. Such gadgets can be found advertised in pet magazines, sold in pet shops, or on the TV. In the UK it is against the Animal Welfare Act to deliberately cause fear and distress to animals, so for this reason qualified behavioural counsellors, quite rightly, would like to see these devices removed from sale.

Whilst visiting a farm I was asked to check out a dog which I was told had started to suffer from seizures, but medication was not helping. The dog looked upset and distressed. Touching her, I felt my throat constrict with a choking sensation. Simultaneously, there was an excruciating explosion throughout my head followed by intense tingling. It was horrible. The poor dog couldn't give me any more clues as to what was going on – she just pleaded with me to sort it. My intuition kicked in, impressing upon me that the dog's problem was not owing to epilepsy, but I couldn't fathom out what it actually was.

It was as I was leaving that I noticed an electric dog collar hanging amongst horse paraphernalia. With horror, I realised that this collar had become faulty, giving the dog frequent electric shocks whenever it was worn, not just when the dog was close to the property's boundary. Urgent checks verified what I suspected and the nasty collar was thrown away – but the innocent dog had already suffered.

Dog sense

It seems that some trainers simply do not understand how dogs think, such as when it comes to a dog's reluctance to walk on shiny or polished floors. A dog with this kind of aversion should not be forced to walk over the surfaces as part of its training, which may include taking rugs away. Let's think about it from a dog's viewpoint.

If we come across a sheet of ice, what do we do? We avoid treading on it. If we choose to go ice skating we can wear special footwear or grab a hand rail to help us balance. Shiny floors are like ice to dogs, and their nails perform the role of skates. Dogs cannot grab onto things with their paws in order to steady themselves and avoid injury, so crossing a slippery or shiny surface is not safe for them and being forced to do so can be very stressful. The joints and muscles of all puppies and dogs are at risk; therefore slippery or polished floors should have rug coverings.

Making a dog move whilst the human is on a bike or skateboard can also create physical problems. Dogs need us to take them out for proper walks and play every day, but they shouldn't be made to move continuously; instead, they should be allowed to stop and sniff things. This enables the dog's muscles and joints to function as they are designed to. Exercise treadmills should only be used after taking advice from an orthopaedic vet, as they can cause injury, mental stress and suffering.

Positive images

Obedience and agility classes can be a lot of fun for dogs. Watching Di, a dog trainer, go through her paces with Blue (the sheltie I look after), I noticed that there was a great deal of communication taking place between them. Body language played a role of course, as did verbal commands. However, sometimes Blue would change direction before Di gave a command, so I talked to Di about what she thought was going on telepathically between them.

Di explained that it is really important to have positive images in our minds of what we want a dog to do and that she was successful in agility competitions because she did this instinctively with Blue. If Blue was having problems on a course, Di would calmly hold images in her mind of how he should proceed. If we become annoyed or distracted, this will send out negative signals to a dog and a trainer must think past any potential problems.

Di always holds the course route in her mind and agreed with me that the minute a handler loses focus their dog will go wrong. In fact from the minute that Di stepped forward to a start line she was focussed on a successful outcome, in her mind's eye seeing the dog go over the jumps smoothly. At every stage, Di sent Blue silent messages such as '*go that way, come left, move right, jump here, slow down, go faster*'.

Dogs understand this kind of mind-to-mind language, loving it when a human is accomplished in this way. Blue had won a major final that summer and Di told me that there was one point in the competition where, owing to the line of a jump, she briefly lost sight of him. When she moved her head slightly they locked eyes again and at that moment she knew without a doubt that they would win. They were both very happy with the round of applause when they accepted their prize, but Blue especially enjoyed his winner's biscuit.

Thinking like a pet

Animal communication is about seeing the world from a pet's perspective and asking, 'If I was this animal how would I feel about this situation, and why?' Animal communication is not about 'making' pets do the things that we want but that may cause them distress.

I once received a query from a person who wanted to know how to persuade a skunk to walk on a lead. The person said that whenever the front door was opened, the skunk froze. I explained that, not surprisingly, the skunk could not cope with such an onslaught of strange smells and noise, which was completely alien to its need for a quiet natural environment.

Letting a cat out into the big wide world can be fraught with problems too, but it is not uncommon for confined cats to become ill owing to their frustration at not being able to use their senses fully in the outside world. A solution for situations in which a cat cannot be left to roam freely is to build a large outdoor area with long grass, shrubs, flowers and climbing frames, or if possible to secure the whole garden. Apartment-dwelling cats should have access to grasses and cat-safe herbs growing in trays and low pots, which they can nibble, smell and sit in. Windows should be opened as much as possible for fresh air, and sunlit places available for the cat to sit in.

Six-year-old Toby suffered from skin problems, which was the reason for my visit. I soon picked up a scene from Toby's mind: a big field spread before me and there was a mouse under my paw. Then this image was repeated over and over again, like a stuck record, and with it came a great sense of longing.

It turned out that a year earlier a visitor to Toby's home had left a window open and housecat Toby had jumped outside. He had been gone for a day and returned at dusk carrying a mouse. It had been the only time in his whole life he had been able to roam and to choose for himself what to do and where to go, a fundamental freedom to the psyche of a cat. The memory of Toby's one happy day was going round and round in his head as he pined to relive it.

I told Toby's owner that he had skin problems because he was depressed and I suggested that she made her garden into a secure cat playground. The woman got on with this project as soon as she could get the builders in – and what a difference it made. Toby's skin condition disappeared within a few weeks of his being free to explore the garden.

The thief

Liz brought her two beagles, Hector and Alfie, to me. They were obviously great pals. As the two dogs tumbled around on top of each other, Liz recounted an amusing story. She had been finding stolen items, such as her personal possessions and small household objects, in Alfie's bed. Whenever Liz puzzled over how they had got into the dog's bed, Hector would watch her, then roll over onto his back, waving his legs in the air. It was all most peculiar. Sometimes she would find Alfie, tail wagging, with one of the items in his mouth. He always looked pleased with himself, even though he was branded a thief.

The mystery was soon solved. Passing by a window, Liz looked in to see Hector take an object from a table and pass it to Alfie, who strutted off with it in his mouth. Hector had been rumbled – he was the real thief. But what was going through his mind? Did Hector want to make Alfie's day, by giving him a gift, or in a cunning way did he want to get him into trouble?

We never did get to the bottom of the mystery, but it shows that we should view animal behaviour as a complex spectrum of thoughts, emotions, action and reaction. There is much for us to enjoy in learning about how the mind of an animal works.

A new pet

When harmony has been established in a household, bringing a new pet into the fold may prove disruptive. When introducing a new member to the family, it's beneficial to send out reassuring thoughts to existing pets. Problems often occur when a human is so focussed on the new pet that the others feel jealous. An old pet can feel cast aside for a younger, healthier animal. In such interactions, try to see the world from all the animals' point of view, including their opinions and possible responses to each other.

It's always stressful for an animal to find itself in a new home, but we can help the process go like clockwork. I got to know TV producer Nikki when she contacted me to appear on the Sky 1 TV programme *Pet Nation*. During a phone call to Nikki, when she had pulled over in her car to speak to me on her mobile, I could hear a cat plaintively crying in the background, saying, 'I'm unsure of what's happening. Am I

🐾 A Helping Paw

When introducing a pet to a new situation try the following:

- 🐾 Imagine bathing pets in pink light to send them love and comfort.
- 🐾 Prepare the existing pets in the household by talking to them about what is going to happen.
- 🐾 Talk to the new arrival about how welcome they are and the fun things you will share, and offer reassurance that you will take care of their needs.
- 🐾 Explain that their role in your life is valuable and irreplaceable.
- 🐾 If you are introducing a pet to the family, explain to each animal that you would like to extend your animal family, and that the new family member will be an addition, not a replacement.
- 🐾 Ask that they share in this additional friendship with you, where you will all be equal.
- 🐾 Hold conversations with animals individually, and as a group.
- 🐾 Send out thoughts of a happy, fun life together.

---

going to be dumped again?' It turned out that the cat, Sparky, was a black stray who had wandered the streets for a year before Nikki had taken in him, originally to shelter him from severe weather. Now Nikki was on her way to see her mum, who had offered Sparky a permanent home.

Following my tips, Nikki explained to Sparky what was going on, and visualised a happy outcome. Nikki's mum got the hang of this too, telling Sparky that although he was eight years old, they could hang out together for many good years. Sparky settled in fantastically, his days of pounding the streets well and truly over

In which Pickle goes off to do his own thing

Through their acute sensitivity, animals read the energy of our moods, which in turn influences their behaviour. Pickle, a Border terrier/Staffordshire terrier cross, is a good example of how this works. He was examining my ankles when his owner Marie announced that he could nip strangers, but thankfully I was spared that form of greeting. Looking down, I admired his dark grey shaggy coat and, although long hair obscured the dog's eyes, every now and again I caught a glimpse of them. They were like sparkly, round black buttons.

We sat on a wooden bench next to an open door in a room alongside a stable block. Marie wanted to know why Pickle had started to nip, so far usually only men. Linking with Pickle, it seemed that he was desperately worried about Marie, which was making him clingy. He nipped men, he said, because Marie subconsciously gave him signals to do so.

The dog had led me into what was potentially a tricky situation. I needed to tread carefully; however, thankfully

Marie opened up about herself without any prompting from me, which is always the best way. She explained that recently her husband had suddenly announced that he no longer loved her and that he had promptly left to live with his mother. Marie had decided to move away from their old home, finding work elsewhere as a housekeeper. A flat and the room we were sitting in came with her new job.

Several times at pertinent points in Marie's story, Pickle looked across at me with a pleading look in his eyes and I detected that he was relieved to be heard. 'I get the picture, Pickle,' I silently transmitted to him. 'This is about her, not you.'

Pickle listened as I told him that I hoped to help Marie feel more positive about her life. It was understandable how she felt as a young woman abandoned by her husband – and with that her sense of security, daily routine and plans for the future had gone too. It was all very hard to cope with. I sensed that Pickle was being overwhelmed by the stress, disruption and uncertainty, and that emotionally his life was also on hold. 'What would you like to do?' I asked him.

Quickly he answered: 'To do things on my own ... but only if Marie is happy with that.'

I communicated that it was my intention to enable him to have his wish. Mary and I talked at length, as I asked all our angels to activate their healing powers. Pickle started to wriggle, clearly wanting to get down and, despite Marie trying to hang onto to him, he jumped off her lap and had a good scratch. Then he had another, followed by more scratching ... and then some more before rolling around on the floor in a frenzy and over my feet. He sprang up and grabbed my right leg with his front paws, rubbing his body along it. Marie was horrified, saying, 'Oh, I'm so embarrassed! He never does this, it's not like he has fleas or worms or anything.'

I laughed, knowing that it was an effect of the healing that had taken place, because healing creates shifts in energy that can produce a temporary tingling sensation. Then Pickle started to run around the room, hunting in the corners before leaping up onto a mattress stacked on a table and nearly pulling it over in the process. Leaping off, he bounced around the room like a hyperactive puppy, knocking things over and generally having fun.

Marie was watching agog. 'What's happening? This is not like Pickle to go off and do things; in fact he's ignoring me!'

Ah Pickle, I thought, *so you've sensed that something has shifted within Marie and that means the burden is lifting from your doggy shoulders.*

Pickle then promptly shot out of the open door and began tearing around the yard. Marie called out, 'Good grief! He never leaves me like that!'

I watched as her dog found a branch in one corner of the yard and, pleased with himself, picked it up in order to carry his prize back to the room. It would be interesting to see what he did with it. Would he present it to Marie? No, he would not. The newly independent Pickle took the branch to the other side of the room and tore it to pieces.

'I can't believe what I'm seeing,' Marie laughed, 'because when I take him out for walks I tell him to run off and to fetch things but he doesn't. He sticks by my side.'

'That,' I answered, 'is because the real message that you actually give Pickle is: "*I am vulnerable, lonely and afraid, so stay with me.*" He reads your heart, not your words. Something has released in you and Pickle senses it. He is showing you that he wants emotional freedom for himself as much as you want yours. This is how much fun he can have, and there is fun ahead for you too.'

It's easy when a woman has been let down by a man for her to hate all the male species (and vice versa); hence Marie's subliminal signals to her dog to nip men when they got too close to her. As Marie set herself free and became less emotionally reliant on Pickle he could stop worrying.

When I left, Pickle was still bouncing around and Marie seemed much more positive. I had a good feeling about them, which turned out to be right. Marie later confirmed that she felt differently about life and Pickle in response was happier – if he could give Marie a paw high-five, I am sure he would.

Pets are in many ways more complex than humans, and it can be difficult for them to fit in with human rules. As these stories show, there is something going on in the mind and heart of an animal all the time. Problems occur if we try to force pets into a preconceived mould of 'perfect' behaviour. Health issues also influence behaviour, which is why the holistic approach is very important in helping a pet stay in tip-top condition. There is a lot that we can do through natural therapies both to prevent problems and to help resolve them if they do occur, so the next chapter will explain in more detail how we can become involved in our pets' lives in this way.

When two worlds meet, learning begins
and our own behaviour can be modified.

12 Caring for Angel Pets

Looking after mind, body and soul.

A pet's health and wellbeing can change in an instant, as can ours. However, at other times problems can arise gradually. If we take a moment to check on our pets every day, this will help us to know what is going on in their lives. I ask my cats, 'How are you feeling?' and I listen to their feedback either in the form of the words I receive, the images or my gut feeling. I also look out for physical indications of discomfort, ill health or unhappiness.

If using the services of an animal communicator, animal healer, or pet behaviourist, bear in mind that reputable ones will not suggest remedies or supplements, owing to their own lack of veterinary training. An animal may be harmed through incorrect advice.

Remember: Our pets are complex characters and, as many different things can go wrong for them, it is absolutely essential that a vet is consulted for an initial diagnosis regarding any concerns we may have.

Once a diagnosis has been made we are then in a position to discuss treatment options, conventional or complementary, with our vet. It is important that we never try to second-guess what is wrong or try complementary therapies at home rather than first take the pet to a vet for professional advice and diagnostic tests.

Signs that need to be investigated by a vet can include:

- Any change in behaviour, e.g. newfound aggression, shyness, reactivity, circling, unusual vocalisation, etc
- Crying, grumbling, lashing out, biting, scratching or snapping when touched, handled or stroked
- Not wanting to play with animal friends, or snapping/lashing out at them
- Withdrawing from contact with humans or other animals
- Sleeping or resting more than normal
- Dull eyes
- Coat looks dull and feels harsh to touch
- Sore mouth or other dental problems; bad breath
- Panting or gasping for breath
- Coughing
- Skin is red/itchy
- Pet is off its food or wants to eat more than normal
- Drinking more or drinking less than usual
- Weight loss or weight gain
- Abnormal vomiting
- Diarrhoea
- Straining when going to the toilet
- Blood in the stools
- Lack of bladder control
- Walking or moving in a different way, including stiffness
- Holding up a paw in discomfort
- Reluctance to go for a walk/exercise
- Reluctance to get into a car or climb stairs
- Pet cries out when moving or getting up
- Licking/biting/scratching/clawing at limbs or the body
- Falling over
- Huddling or feathers falling out for birds

… and anything else that you are concerned about.

Dogs show signs of pain more readily than cats, and with older cats we have to be especially vigilant because although they tend to sleep more as they get older, they may be resting more than usual owing to discomfort from arthritis or other problems.

Emotional pain

Reading my newspaper one morning, I noticed a report about a university lecturer who suggested that animals should be genetically bred so that they don't feel pain, the idea being that their lives in factory farms would be more ethically acceptable to us. I found this a strange concept because pain, of course, can be emotional as well as physical. The animals would still be stressed by their lifestyle and laboratory animals would still know that they were having procedures done to them. Emotional pain in pets – which may have a variety of causes including grief, abuse and neglect, or loss of a home or a companion – is very real, and natural therapies can help a pet to overcome it. As with humans, emotional problems can be at the heart of many physical diseases and illness will also trigger emotional distress.

However, I am concerned that a pet antidepressant has been approved for sale. Rather than give a pet a chemical cosh for behaving in a way that demonstrates he or she is suffering from a problem, we owe it to the animal to get to the bottom of what is wrong. How ridiculous to read that the drug company said that it was helping to restore the human–pet bond. Finding out what is wrong and making changes to alleviate a pet's emotional, mental or physical distress is what helps the bond.

I agree with Roger Mugford, an animal psychologist, who says: 'Most breakthroughs in dog behaviour are achieved by carrying a titbit and using it wisely, not by drugs.'

A pet is what it eats

Diet is one of the fundamental areas of pet care. Holistic vets encourage feeding pets fresh natural foodstuffs both to help prevent illness and to improve the health of sick animals. We have become over-reliant on purchased pet foods, many of which contain poor quality ingredients and toxic additives. Processed pet food is linked to health problems, particularly skin and bowel. If we feed a pet dry food (kibble) and nothing else, or with just a bit of tinned food added, we are not giving it a healthy diet. This kind of food does not allow cat and dog digestive systems to do the job they are designed for – i.e. to process a variety of raw foods. Cats and dogs have sensitive taste buds so how boring must it be for them to be given a bowl of dry food day in and day out? Fresh meat, preferably organic, also has the added benefit of cleaning dogs' and cats' teeth. Many holistic vets have easy-to-make recipes for pets on their websites.

Feeding only a dry diet to rabbits leads to painful teeth problems as well as gut disease. Muesli mix foods are fattening. Rabbits need to eat grass as the silicates in the blades help wear the teeth down. They must have fresh good-quality hay at all times, topped up with some fresh seasonal vegetables, leaves and herbs. Runs – which should be at least four metres long – need to be moved around the garden to ensure a constant supply of fresh grass. Mown grass should not be fed to them as it rapidly ferments and the use of chemicals in the garden also should be avoided due to toxic residues.

I interviewed holistic vet Nick Thompson, who has a special interest in diet, about the difference food changes can make to a dog or cat's wellbeing. He told me about Maggie, a three-year-old Welsh terrier, who had been visiting the vet for bowel, skin and ear problems every fortnight from the time

Rabbits need a healthy diet.

she had been a puppy. Neither antibiotics nor steroids made the slightest difference and the poor little dog continued to suffer. Then the owners consulted Nick, who immediately changed Maggie's diet to home-made food. Within six weeks Maggie was perfectly healthy for the first time in her life. So impressed were the owners that they gave up their jobs and started a raw pet food company, so that other animals could enjoy better health.

Half an hour after eating his dried food, two-year-old English bull terrier Chester would perform the 'wall of death' by racing manically around the edges of the room. He also suffered from chronic bowel problems, which special veterinary prescribed diets did not resolve. Within two weeks of his being put on a natural diet Chester was a changed dog. Now after eating he chills out, his mad racing activity a thing of the past.

'Dangerous' Dave is a stunning Abyssinian tomcat, whom Nick describes as being the colour of a tawny nut with black ticking to the tips of his fur. The cat got his nickname due to his highly active nature, not through any aggressive traits, but he was a sick cat. Dave had chronic bloody diarrhoea when his very worried owner brought him to Nick. The conventional approach had been steroids, which were unsuccessful, but when Nick changed Dave's diet he was cured within two weeks.

Excessive limb-licking is often seen in cats and dogs. Molly, an eight- year-old Westie, was very itchy and had licked her feet raw. In fact, when Nick saw Molly, her feet were a burgundy colour from the soreness. High doses of steroids had made Molly's plight worse, as they caused her to drink and urinate uncontrollably. Changing her diet brought about an improvement, and over the next three months her feet became whiter and whiter as the itching ceased.

Sometimes a suffering pet may be on the verge of being put to sleep, having been labelled 'incurable'. Three-year-old lurcher Sol had irritable bowel syndrome every day of his life and would curl up in misery because of the pain. As a last resort, the owner came to Nick and he devised a fresh diet for Sol, who improved within a week and was totally cured in a month.

These stories illustrate how much damage a junk diet can do to a pet's health, and how easy it is for us to do something about it.

🐾 www.holisticvet.co.uk – downloadable natural recipes
🐾 www.naturalinstinct.com – raw pet food supplies

Also see:
🐾 www.BAHVS.com, www.ahvma.org and www.viim.org

The holistic care package

Conventional veterinary care is essential in many cases, and I have relied on it for treating my own pets' acute conditions and for giving them life-saving emergency treatment, as well as essential surgery. However, it could be argued that conventional medicine is less successful in dealing with chronic problems that keep reoccurring once a drugs regimen has been stopped. Drugs also have side effects that can produce additional problems.

The holistic aim is to return animals to good health without the use of drugs or invasive treatments. The beauty of talking to a qualified vet who is also trained in other therapies, is that you can get the best of both orthodox and alternative medicine. Holistic vets have taken further training in homeopathy, herbal medicine, nutrition and acupuncture, for example. Holistic vets also tend to allow more time than conventional vets for a detailed consultation and will want to treat the whole animal, not just symptoms. During a consultation with a holistic vet, in order to help work out the best treatment options for the pet, questions will be asked about the animal's personality and background, diet, lifestyle, environment/household, family circumstances, exercise regime and behaviour, for instance.

Interest in the holistic approach is thankfully increasing as people seek to avoid medication side effects both for themselves and their pets. Holistic therapies can usually be safely used alongside essential conventional medical treatments, offering the patient the best of both worlds.

Bringing the pet into the loop

If your pet is involved in an emergency or has a condition that requires urgent attention, then it is essential that you consult a normal vet immediately. Where possible, I will also seek follow-up advice from a holistic vet to see what other non-invasive options and alternatives are available. With chronic conditions, I prefer to use remedies that will do no long-term harm.

Animals possess an inner wisdom about what is right or wrong for them and I believe that it is important to bring the pet into the decision-making loop when it comes to settling on the best course of treatment. Absorbing a pet's energy and blending with them, I say to myself: *'I am this animal, so what do I want to happen to me, what feels right for me?'* I then allow my sixth sense and intuition to help me make an informed decision, as I did with Mitzi when she developed cancer. I find this makes it easier for me to make a judgement about the correct treatment to offer the pet. I keep the communication dialogue going with the pet throughout a course of treatment, and make daily checks as to how it is feeling, and if there are any changes that I should be making or if there is anything else that I can do to help. It's very important to check any decision we make with a vet so that the animal does not suffer or miss out on the right help.

Teddy's miraculous recovery

When Lilly ran past me flashing the message that her brother Teddy was in serious trouble, my mouth went dry and my heart raced. Running outside, I heard two neighbours' young sons on their bicycles yelling, 'Let's get the cat!' Teddy then crawled through a hedge, dragging his back legs. X-rays later showed that he had a complicated fracture to the right hip joint caused by impact, as well as severe spinal bruising. The local orthopaedic vet wanted to amputate the leg and I was in shock.

Quickly, though, I gathered my contacts together and came up with a plan of action. Driving three hours, I took Teddy to a referral specialist veterinary hospital, where a top surgeon operated on him and, inserting pins, managed to save his leg. I was thrilled that Teddy had benefited from this surgeon's expertise, but was warned that there was a fairly high risk that the operation might prove a failure; that Teddy would have to endure at least twelve weeks' cage confinement; and that most likely, if the pins held, he would be left with a permanent limp.

Once I had taken Teddy home after the op, his holistic team swung into action. As well as nursing Teddy, I gave him healing treatments every few hours. My colleague Amanda Sutton, the renowned chartered veterinary physiotherapist, came two days later and started laser treatment to help speed wound repair. She also did some gentle therapy to help ease Teddy's sore muscles. Homeopathic remedies had been started before the operation, and Nick Thompson made home visits to give Teddy acupuncture treatments.

Six weeks later the check-up day came and Teddy was driven back to the surgeon for an X-ray that would reveal what his future was to be. 'It's a miracle,' the beaming vet said as he returned Teddy from the examination room. 'I can't believe that the bone has completely repaired in such a short time. Not only that, Teddy is walking normally, as if nothing had happened to him.' Teddy was discharged and didn't spend any more time in the cage, although I did restrict his activity for a few months to make sure he was really strong and the holistic treatments continued for several more months.

This all took place seven years ago, and now Teddy is the most agile cat I have ever had. Holistic teamwork like this makes all the difference, because the pet benefits from everyone's skills.

A last resort

American holistic vet Dr Marcie Fallek has discussed numerous successes with me, one of which was featured in the *New York Times*. Chloe, a five-year-old golden retriever mix, had been hit by a car, which left her with a broken back that involved displaced vertebrae. The poor dog was screaming in pain and completely paralysed, with no bladder or bowel control. Marcie treated Chloe three times a week with acupuncture and some remedies. After the second acupuncture treatment, Chloe wagged her tail. Improving with each session, Chloe was back to normal after only ten treatments.

When Chloe's owners took her back to the clinic where her condition had originally been diagnosed, the surgeons were amazed. A follow-up X-ray confirmed that the dog's back was completely healed and there was no longer any vertebrae displacement. Marcie saw Chloe again ten years later to treat her for Cushing's disease, and she learned that the dog's back had never given her any problems. Marcie initially had no idea if she could help Chloe, who would have been euthanised if treatment had failed. The success was attributed to Chloe being a young healthy dog with an acute traumatic injury that was immediately holistically addressed.

What natural remedies can help a pet?

Homeopathy

Homeopathy is used by millions of people around the world, and for many animals too. Organic farmers rely on homeopathic remedies as an effective yet safe alternative to drugs, as they leave no unwanted residues in milk, meat or eggs.

Homeopathy is a therapy that treats the mind as well as the whole body, not just the symptoms. Homeopathy relies on the energy of a remedy to work with the animal's individual vital force to aid the natural healing process, and homeopathic vets will take a detailed history so that they can match the right remedy and dose to the individual animal. Homeopathy is safe for all ages and all species; it can help treat many conditions including tumours, heart, kidney and liver problems, skin problems, epilepsy, poor immune system, shock, grief, and chronic illness.

I asked holistic vet Cheryl Sears for some examples of cases where natural therapies had made a real difference to pets. Cheryl told me about fourteen-year-old Jimmy, a black cat with very bad arthritis of the spine, calcified discs in the lower spine and degenerative joint disease in both hips. Jimmy had been treated with non-steroidal anti-inflammatory medication and responded well to physiotherapy. Cheryl started acupuncture, giving one treatment a month for the past two and a half years, and also put Jimmy onto a daily homeopathic remedy. As a result Jimmy is active and mobile, and there has been no need to use conventional medication for his condition.

Texas is an American cocker spaniel who was first brought to see Cheryl when he was four years old. What a sorry state Texas was in. The dog had severe skin problems which were so bad that all four feet were swollen, with discharging cysts between the pads. There were also big red spots under his forelegs and in the groin area. Texas's condition had been diagnosed as an allergy to an unknown cause which was overwhelming his immune system. Texas had been on daily steroids and antibiotics for nine months when his owner consulted Cheryl. Over a few months, a number of homeopathic remedies were selected by Cheryl based on the dog's character and symptoms. Texas is now given only one remedy twice a week, and there are no lesions on his skin.

In the UK, it is the law that only a vet may prescribe homeo-pathic remedies for animals. In other countries without this restriction, I still advise people to use someone with veteri-nary training rather than a lay person, in order to safeguard the animal's health and wellbeing. There are some good self-help books available which offer advice on easing minor conditions, once a vet has made a professional diagnosis.

For further information see:

❧ www.BAHVS.com – the British Association of Homeo-pathic Veterinary Surgeons

❧ For the US see: www.ahvma.org – the American Holistic Veterinary Medical Association, and www.viim.org – the Veterinary Institute of Integrated Medicine

Herbs

Veterinary herbal medicine is as old as human herbal medi-cine and is used to treat a wide range of ailments as well as to promote good health. Some trained holistic vets can prescribe herbs for medicinal purposes as an alternative to drugs, as well as give advice on which herbs to offer pets in their food. When considering using herbs for pets, it is essen-tial to take advice first from a holistic vet about which herbs might be suitable in order to avoid creating a fresh problem or making an existing one worse. Cats can be particularly sensitive to herb toxicity. Herbs should be grown organically to avoid chemical residues being taken into the pet's system.

In the UK only a vet may prescribe herbs for animals.

For further information see:

❧ In the UK, the British Association of Veterinary Herbalists at www.herbalvets.org.uk

❧ In the USA, the Veterinary Botanical Medicine Association at www.vbma.org

Acupuncture

When performed by a qualified veterinary acupuncturist, acupuncture is safe and can be very effective with animals. It is mostly practised on dogs, cats, and horses but many other species can benefit, including birds, rabbits and guinea pigs. Pets can be treated with acupuncture for a wide range of conditions, including joint problems, neck and back problems, muscle spasms, pain and inflammation, lameness, arthritis, nerve problems, paralysis, wounds, eye conditions, skin conditions and for pain relief after surgery or accidents. In female dogs and cats acupuncture can help with urinary incontinence.

During an acupuncture treatment very fine needles are inserted over specific points, but for nervous or sensitive animals a laser stimulation pen can be used instead. I frequently suggest to clients that they consult an acupuncture vet. This is because I have found it so successful with my own animals over the years, and I like the fact that there are no side effects, only side benefits.

Note: in the UK only a vet may administer acupuncture to animals

For further information see:
- 🐾 The Association of British Veterinary Acupuncturists at www.abva.co.uk
- 🐾 The International Veterinary Acupuncture Society at www.ivas.org

Physiotherapy

The purpose of physiotherapy is to restore and maintain mobility, function, independence and performance. Chartered animal physiotherapists can check the muscles and the skeletal system, as well as prescribe exercises. All animals can respond to physiotherapy and it is commonly used with dogs, cats and horses. Many chartered animal physiotherapists now have a Master's degree in veterinary physiotherapy from the Royal Veterinary College, which is recognised worldwide as a measure of excellence. In the US the letters PT after a person's name is an indication of professional training in this field.

As well as using their hands, animal physiotherapists may also use a range of electrical equipment, including lasers and ultrasound. Conditions that can respond to animal physiotherapy include: joint problems, lameness, neck/back/shoulder problems, arthritis, falls, discomfort after surgery or accidents, and age-related weakness/stiffness.

A hydrotherapy pool should be used with dogs only following a consultation with a chartered animal physiotherapist, as there are conditions which can be aggravated, or even created, by swimming. Dogs who take part in agility or other sports can benefit from physiotherapy in order to nip any problems in the bud and keep them in tiptop condition.

Tom, the comedian dog, sometimes has accidents owing to his being so boisterous. One day, Tom communicated to me that his neck was sore so I asked him how this had come about. Quickly, I picked up an image of Tom hurtling through the air, down a flight of steps, and then skidding at the bottom into a heap. I discussed this mishap with his owner Debbie, who informed me that at the back of her house is a door opening onto a patio area which has steps down to the lawn. Whenever the door was opened Tom had got into the habit of pushing past the other dogs and leaping in the air, over the steps and onto the grass. Then he would run to the bottom of the long garden like a mad thing looking for whatever unfortunate rabbits or squirrels happened to be around. On the morning of the incident, there had been a frost and when Tom ran out of the door he had skidded – hence the fall.

That is one of the great things about tuning into animals: we can pick up problems that would otherwise go unheeded. Without the right treatment Tom could end up with lameness, so I thanked him for letting us know about his damaged muscles. A few days later he had physiotherapy, which sorted out his injury before it became a major issue.

On another occasion, Tom transmitted information about falling over an agility jump during a competition and hurting his shoulder. When I asked him what had caused the tumble, he didn't answer for a few seconds. It seemed he was mulling over his answer. Tom then communicated that he'd been running rather fast around the course and one of the obstacles had been in his way. Debbie clarified that what had actually happened was that Tom had been playing the fool, hectically running around instead of paying attention to her commands, and hurtling over the jumps. In doing so he clipped the top of one and fell in a heap at the bottom of it. So Tom went back to the physiotherapist for more treatment.

Cats have their own 'agility classes' as they go about their daily lives jumping and climbing. This can lead to injuries, and cats suffer from ageing joint problems too. When necessary, and after a veterinary diagnosis, physiotherapy can help cats maintain mobility and help alleviate discomfort.

❧ If you are interested in physiotherapy for any animal see www.acpat.org

❧ For the USA see http://www.orthopt.org/sig_apt.php

Healing

As the stories in this book show, healing and animal communication go hand in hand. Tuning into healing energy helps us therefore to monitor what our pets are saying.

Around the world there is a growing interest in healing, i.e. channelling beneficial energy using the hands. Everyone has the potential to do this, as my books *Hands-on Healing for Pets* and *Healing for Horses* explain. Healing is the only therapy that reaches the soul level and it can help mentally, emotionally and physically. However, promises of a cure can never be given, as each case is unique and depends on many factors, and – like other therapies – healing is not a miracle cure-all. Healing is very rewarding to give, is safe to use alongside veterinary treatment and can be given to animals of any age. Pets love healing, so I encourage everyone to have a go at it themselves.

When animals know that we can communicate with them – in other words, that we can hear what they say, sense how they are feeling and even offer them healing – they will make special efforts to spend time with us. The hairdresser that I use has her salon attached to her house; one day as I was having my hair done, there was a commotion and a dog burst into the room, ran up to me and sat pressed against my leg. The hairdresser stood motionless, scissors in her hand, staring at the dog, and then said: 'I can't believe what I am seeing here. This is my neighbour's dog, he's a rescue and nervous of people. The only way he can have got here was to jump the fence. It looks like he came especially to be with you.' And of course I knew that he had. Over the airwaves, he had sensed that I was close by and with great excitement he had come round for a chat. As my hair was snipped, information flowed from the dog. He wanted to unburden himself about his past and tell me how he felt now. He explained that his heart was a bit weak, so he wondered if I could lay my healing hands on him. After a while the dog yawned and, going to the door, asked to be taken back to his people.

Edith asks for healing help

Through the universal consciousness animals can communicate a need for healing any time and anywhere. A good example of this took place when I was teaching at the Open Center in New York. Working with a red colour shih-tzu called Gibby, I suddenly heard him communicate the name of Edith. I asked Gibby's owner if she could shed some light on who Edith was, feeling that it was another dog, but she could not. So I put the same question to the class and as I did so the name seemed to hover over the middle of the group of people watching me. A hand shot up and a woman called Helen said, 'Edith is a pug that I recently fostered, but as far as I know she is fine.' When I looked down at Gibby, he communicated to me that all was not well with Edith, so I asked the class to join me in sending healing thoughts to her.

Arriving back in the UK, I received an email from Helen, updating me on Edith. Checking with the dog's adopter about what I had picked up, Helen had learnt that Edith had that very week developed a bad problem in her hips, restricting her climbing stairs. The adopter thanked us for sending out the healing thoughts and booked Edith in at the vet's. She did recover, however, a few days later.

What astonished me is that Gibby had never met Edith, but somehow he knew that Edith needed help ... and Edith had tuned into our healing energy from her home some miles away, knowing that we could help her. Animals know more than we do in many respects and we should always bear this in mind and learn what we can from it.

To the same class, Thurman had brought along the sweetest little Chihuahua called Taco. He was around six years old and for the first two years of his life had been confined to a small box with another dog. When Thurman adopted Taco and took him home with her he had never been on a lead or felt grass under his paws. I was told that Taco was very nervous of strangers, so I took great care to reassure him as that day nearly sixty people were watching me demonstrate healing with several dogs. Thurman sat next to me with Taco on her lap and, touching him, I instigated a healing soul conversation. At first, the little dog leant on his 'mum' but several minutes later something suddenly changed and there was an audible murmur from people watching as they noticed it happening. Taco stopped shivering and sat upright, looking alert and happy. His ears pricked, he yawned several times, and then he licked my fingers, as if to reward them for healing him. He looked like a different dog. Many of those present, including myself, shed a tear at that.

Later Thurman sought me out to thank me for helping Taco. I thanked her for bringing him because he was one of my animal teachers that day. We can acquire a great deal of knowledge about the power of healing energy from every animal we meet.

🐾 For information about courses and healer training worldwide see: www.thehealingtrust.org.uk

Pet behaviour counselling

A 'behavioural problem' is an animal acting in a particular way because it is trying to communicate something. With expert help we can usually sort these kinds of problems out.

Qualified behaviour counsellors work in veterinary practices or make home visits to help with pet problems. The range of behavioural problems exhibited in companion animals is varied and may include: aggression, destructiveness, toileting problems, marking, spraying, self-mutilation, vocal behaviour, nervousness, problems with car travel, livestock chasing and generally being out of control. Professionally qualified animal behaviour counsellors can offer help with these and any other behaviour problems.

A consultation in your home should last around two hours or more, and a detailed history will be taken, including species type, breed, genetics, age of pet, sex, and when the problem started. Diet is also discussed as it affects behaviour. An analysis will be made to help the practitioner to work out what is going on, and the consultant should also liaise with the veterinary profession. Suggestions will be made as to how to manage the situation followed by phone calls and further visits as necessary.

These websites give information on how to find professionally trained animal behavioural counsellors:

🐾 www.apbc.org.uk
🐾 www.animalbehaviorcounselors.org

Other Useful information

Books on dog training and behaviour

David Appleby, *Ain't Misbehavin'*, Broadcast Books, 1998 (ISBN 9781874092728)

Jean Donaldson, *The Culture Clash*, James Kenneth, 1996 (ISBN 978-1888047059)

Barry Eaton, *Dominance: Fact or Fiction?* Barry Eaton, 2008 (ISBN 978-0953303946)

Kendal Shepherd, *The Canine Commandments*, Broadcast Books, 2007 (ISBN 978-1874092551)

Cat and rabbit books

Sarah Heath, *Why Does My Cat ...?* Souvenir Press, 2000 (ISBN 9780285635494)

Anne McBride, *Why Does My Rabbit ...?* Souvenir Press, 2000 (ISBN 978-0285635500)

Books about understanding animals

Marc Bekoff, *The Animal Manifesto*, New World Library, 2010 (ISBN 978-1577316497)

—*The Emotional Lives of Animals*, New World Library, 2008 (ISBN 978-1577316299)

Leslie Irvine, *If You Tame Me: Understanding Our Connection with Animals,* Temple University Press, 2004 (ISBN 978-1592132446)

Books on natural remedies for pets

Richard Allport, *Natural Healthcare for Pets*, Element Books, 2001 (ISBN 978-0007130870)

—*Heal Your Dog the Natural Way*, Remember When, 2010 (ISBN 978-1844681105)

Dr Ian Billinghurst, *The Barf Diet*, 2001 (ISBN 978-095892512)

Christopher Day, *The Homeopathic Treatment of Small Animals*, Rider and Co, 2005 (ISBN 978-1844132898)

Don Hamilton, *Homeopathic Care for Cats and Dogs,* North Atlantic Books, 2000 (ISBN 978-1556432958)

George Macleod, *Homeopathic Remedies for Cats*, Rider and Co, 2005 (ISBN 978-1844131945)

George Macleod, *Homeopathic Remedies for Dogs*, Rider and Co, 2005 (ISBN 978-1844131969)

Clare Middle, *Real Food for Cats and Dogs*, Freemantle Press, 2008 (ISBN 978-1921361357)

Kymythy Schultze, *Natural Nutrition for Dogs and Cats – the Ultimate Diet*, Hay House, 2003 (ISBN 978-1561706365)

Martin Zucker, *Veterinarians' Guide to Natural Remedies for Cats*, Crown Publishing, 2000 (ISBN 978-0609803738)

Music for Pets

I have collaborated on four CDs of relaxing music suitable for playing to pets and horses. These include the titles: *Animal Healing, Music for Pets, Animal Angels* and *Connecting with Animals*. My instructional DVD entitled 'Animal Healing' on how to channel healing energy to animals is also available.

Available worldwide from New World Music:
www.newworldmusic.com
From UK telephone 01986 891600
Non-UK telephone 0044 1986 891600
USA telephone number 800 771 0987

All items available in the UK from Margrit Coates, www.theanimalhealer.com

13. When Dreams Come True

Angel pets illuminate our vision

During sleep, the language of the brain is said to be symbolic, so a dream can have a meaning beyond an obvious interpretation. Dreams can sometimes bring important messages and mine frequently feature animals, who bring me insights and inspiration. Sometimes, I wake in the middle of a dream having been given words. Quickly, I write down these gems of spiritual wisdom before I go back to sleep, hoping for more.

When we sleep our chattering mind is set aside, and our soul can explore other dimensions. Therefore it can be easier for guardian angels to give us feedback on what we need to know. That is why so often people wake up with solutions to problems. If a pet is talking to us as we wake up, before our everyday mind takes over, then it is a time when we can hear them more clearly.

'Do you need more sleep?' asked the cat

Nicole Golding and Adam Goodfellow are natural horsemanship trainers who invariably fall into bed exhausted after a hard day's work. One winter Nicole had booked herself to go on a riding clinic and was really looking forward to it. When her alarm went off early on the day of the clinic it was still dark outside. As Nicole was surfacing from a deep sleep her cat, Professor Smidgeon, placed his paw onto her arm, and Nicole felt an instant flash of warmth flood throughout her body. Nicole distinctly heard Professor Smidgeon say to her, 'You seem very tired; are you sure you need to get up now?'

Nicole assured Professor Smidgeon that she did indeed want to get up at that time, but she thanked him for his concern. Nicole tells me that she had never heard Professor Smidgeon communicate anything in this way to her before, and it has not occurred since. It's interesting that although Nicole felt ready to get up, her cat read her energy and thought that she was not rested enough, hence his concern. It seems to me that, time and again, the evidence is there that pets read us on a very deep level and in doing so try to use that information in a way that is beneficial way for us.

Heart to heart

There was a profound dream-link I had once with my cat Floyd, a beautiful blue-grey shorthair. He was Mitzi's son, whom I first met when he was three weeks old, and now aged nine he lay in a veterinary hospital, his life hanging in the balance.

Floyd had seemed to be a healthy cat, but every now and again he would lose some weight, before gaining it again. Naturally, I had Floyd checked over by various vets, but they were not unduly worried, as his coat was shiny, his temperature normal and he had bags of energy. Intuitively, though, I knew that something was very wrong, but running my hands over Floyd I could not pinpoint where the problem was originating from. I would ask Floyd if he felt unwell, and apart from sometimes communicating a feeling of nausea, he said he was OK.

I loved Floyd with a passion. We shared conversations about anything and everything. Floyd helped me overcome obstacles and transitions in my life with his enthusiasm, wisdom, knowing, playfulness and – oh yes, his love. When I held him in my arms he melted into me and we became one. Floyd encouraged me to be fully in tune with my spiritual essence.

It all came to a standstill the day that I found Floyd slumped in the corner of a room and he squealed when I touched his body. By the time I got to the veterinary clinic, Floyd's eyeballs were bloodshot and he was hot to the touch.

The vet was a locum and very thorough with his examination. 'Something is bugging me about this case,' he told me as he scrolled through Floyd's case notes on the computer. 'I need to urgently send blood to the lab for some specific tests to be run.'

Jabs were administered and I took Floyd back home, where I placed him on my bed – his favourite sleeping place. He was groggy from the medication and all night long I kept vigil whilst holding my finger on the tip of his paw, his body too sore to be touched. The next morning Floyd took a turn for the worse and I took him back to the vet, and from there he was sent to the veterinary hospital. I was shocked when Floyd was placed in an isolation cubicle because they suspected a viral disease called FIP – feline infectious peritonitis – which is invariably fatal. It was suspected that Floyd had carried the disease from birth, but regular healing from me was the reason why his immune system had been so strong for many years.

It would be a while before the test results came back and so each morning I went to the hospital where I sat on the floor by Floyd's cubicle. When I opened the door he would crawl out, dragging his drip tubes, to lie across my lap. As I gently caressed Floyd's head I spoke softly to him, talking about our time together, recalling things that had happened over the years. As I spoke I knew that my memories spun golden images through my mind and into Floyd's. Through our affection for each other, we became one heart, beating in unison and remembering a life shared and full of love.

I would then go home for a while, before returning in the evening and later falling into bed exhausted. After a few days of this routine the head vet spoke to me as I left, saying, 'Tomorrow we get the results, but I'm pretty sure it's the virus.' At this remark, I went back to look at Floyd. I noticed that he was curled like a crescent moon, one front paw crossed over the other, his head tilted slightly, his eyes half closed. At the sight of his innocence, my heart flew out of my chest and lay in the cubicle next to Floyd.

A lot goes through your mind at a time like this, including guilt at remembering your less than perfect ways, when you were impatient instead of giving your pet a cuddle. How you wish you could turn back the clock. I was too self-absorbed to be able to tune into Floyd at that moment and, leaving the building, I left him to his fitful dozing.

That night I dreamt of Floyd. Or rather I dreamt of myself, because it seemed that we were one being, and in this dream I had my own thoughts but whenever I looked down at my body it was Floyd's. I held up my hands and they were paws – my feet were covered in hair and had claws. In my dream I was not afraid but understood this phenomenon perfectly. Everything throughout the universe is part of a whole and perhaps all creatures are fragments of each other, connected and joined together like a giant spider's web. In this dream there was no beginning, no end, and no separation, just an all-consuming insight that I knew the reason why everything happened. There is a divine order.

On waking I felt something move off my chest, but looking down there was nothing there. I knew then that Floyd had actually been with me during the night, our hearts entwined through the powerful connection that we can have with an angel. During that long night we had been healing each other, knowing what the fullness of morning was to bring.

That day I cradled Floyd as the vet ended his suffering. A circular buzzing sensation tapped my palms. It was Floyd's soul departing for the afterlife. Through our dream connection it was what Floyd and I had prepared each other for. It didn't lessen my pain, though, and the embarrassed vet left me to wail and sob as I huddled over Floyd, his physical life extinguished, his body growing cold and stiff in my hands.

That night, I had another dream. Floyd and I were dancing, a waltzing couple twirling round and round in a pool of pure white light. It was the healing dance.

The angel lady's cat

When I discussed the topic of pets and dreams with my friend the award-winning author Jacky Newcomb, she told me about her own intriguing story.

She explained: 'I woke from a powerful dream one night knowing that we would soon be the owners of a new cat. When I walked into the kitchen for breakfast that morning, my youngest daughter was already at the table. "Mum, I had a dream …" she began confidently, "I dreamt we had a ginger kitten and it was chasing a butterfly …." Bizarrely, we'd both had dreams about a kitten on the same night. This was surely more than a coincidence?

'So that was it, the deal was sealed – somewhere, someone had decided we needed a cat in our lives. I'd sensed the cat was to be a male and began the search by ringing round all the local rescue centres. Someone eventually called me back: "We have three kittens: a black female and two male ginger tomcats ...."

'We arranged to call at the rescue "foster home" that very afternoon. I knew it was likely that "our cat" was going to be one of the two toms. When my husband John, our two daughters and I finally arrived, we were led outside to where the three kittens and their mother were being held. The foster mum told us that the mother cat was feral and her kittens had been born in the wild. The kittens seemed terrified of our presence, but I knew that a little patience and time would be all that was needed. Of the two male cats, one had a serious infection and was not ready to be re-homed, so that left only one ginger tomcat – who had to be "our cat".

'Later that week, we brought Tigger home. As we pulled into the drive, I spotted a white butterfly in the garden. It was the first one I'd seen all year ... and just like in my daughter's dream.

'Not long after Tigger had turned old enough to go out into the garden during daylight hours, he disappeared. Instinct immediately told me something was wrong, and when my sister called round later she was bemused. "But how long has he been gone?" she asked. "An hour ..." I answered but my gut feeling told me he wasn't coming back any time soon.

'I hunted high and low, but a week later he still hadn't appeared. I began to have regular dreams about my precious pet and knew that Tigger was shut in somewhere. I printed posters and leaflets, and started knocking on doors all over the village. Yet Tigger was still nowhere to be found.

'In the meantime my nightmares grew in intensity. One night I dreamt that Tigger was on the doorstep of a house about half a mile away. I knew the house and called the following morning with tears in my eyes. The homeowner wasn't a cat fan and wasn't sympathetic. If Tigger *had* been here he wasn't now; however, another neighbour in the area told me she'd seen a ginger kitten a few days earlier when she had been walking her dogs. It gave me renewed hope.

'My brother-in-law had a dream about Tigger too. He told my sister upon waking: 'Tigger was walking across the field with a fox … he's been on a great adventure.'

'Then a friend put to me the million-dollar question: "Jacky, don't you teach people to ask their guardian angels for help with things like this?" I do … but in this case I hadn't taken my own advice! That night, before I went to bed I sat down with a pen and paper. I wrote: "Angels, please bring home my darling cat, Tigger …" That night I had a dream in which a man called at the door with two cats in his hands … he was delivering the pets back to their owners. And one of the cats was Tigger! I felt sure this was a sign.

'I woke up the following morning full of joy. Sure enough, that weekend my mobile phone rang. I heard a woman say, "Mrs Newcomb? I have your cat here …" The lady explained that she'd spotted Tigger in her garden a week earlier, before travelling to her other house, which was several hundred miles away. When she returned home the following week she noticed the "stray" cat in her garden once more. A trip to the local shop had meant she'd seen my poster … and instantly recognised him.

'I arranged for my parents to collect Tigger for me … my dad becoming the "angel" in the dream who returned him to my house. We bought Tigger a whole chicken as his welcome-home gift. He did nothing but purr and eat for a week. Strangely his white "socks" paws were now bright pink … it looked as if Tigger had spent many hours trying to dig his way out of somewhere so I guess he had been shut in, just as he'd shown me in my dream.'

Jacky went on to tell me that she had found a new friend for Tigger. Magik is a cheeky black kitten ... and of course Jacky first saw her in a dream too.

A soul kiss

There is a saying 'go to bed and sleep on it', meaning that if we have a problem or decision to make the answer will come to us during the night so that we will know it when we wake. In a similar way, we can 'go to bed and talk with the animals'. We can meet angel animal messengers in our dreams.

Animals have their dreams too. I leave you for now with three stories which epitomise just how powerful a soul conversation with a pet can be, and which show how these conversations can lead to miraculous outcomes.

As I mentioned earlier in the story about the amazing saviour rabbit, Twinkle, I met 'bunny lady' Adele when I was filming for *Animal Roadshow*. Adele had brought along with her seven-year-old Rupert, a white Angora rabbit, who had dark silver tips to the fur around his neck and eyes. Rupert had been kept in a two foot by two foot box in a cellar until Adele took him away from this hellhole. He had been found at a fur farm, where he had only been taken out of the box to be combed, his fur being used to make angora garments.

As a result of his incarceration, Rupert had terrible muscle-wasting – not to mention severe depression. As soon as Adele had rescued Rupert she presented him with space, but he didn't know how to use it. This poor creature had suffered physical and psychological damage that kept him literally rooted to the spot. Adele has a group of bunnies in her house and Rupert accepted having them around him, but did not indulge in usual bunny behaviour, nor would he follow the other rabbits into the outdoor area.

Eventually Rupert started to creep out from inside his play-house, but he soon darted back into it again. Picking him up, Adele tried to place Rupert outside in the garden area but whenever she did he would panic and dash back inside. There was something special about Rupert, though, and Adele desperately wanted to be able to help him recover from his ordeal and enjoy his new life. Seeing an advert that invited people to appear on *Animal Roadshow* with me, Adele called the number. By now Rupert had been with her for six months and he still needed all the help he could get.

Animals can suffer from post-traumatic stress syndrome just like humans do and this sweet bunny was clearly in a bad way. As I chatted to Adele over the carrier that contained Rupert, I also made telepathic contact with him, throwing him a healing lifeline. I felt a sensation cross my face like a soft breath. I looked up at the camera crew and production team to see if this phenomenon came from them or their equipment. It did not. There it was again, a sensation across my right cheek. Rupert's twitching nose appeared from the carrier and, as he ventured out, I knew that the sensation was being transmitted from him. Of course he was not actually blowing at me; it was his soul energy that I could feel as he began to communicate. A soul kiss.

Bending down, I scooped Rupert up into my arms. 'Hello, Rupert,' I said, and then a very small, almost inaudible voice shyly whispered back, 'Hello.'

All this took place in the space of a couple of minutes and whilst it was going on I had an audience. For the TV programme I had to talk as soon as I was introduced to the animals, asking questions, saying what I was picking up from them, making observations and explaining what the animals were communicating to me and how. Then to finish off I would give the animals some healing. There was always one thing going on silently between myself and the animals, and a separate verbal explanation coming out of my mouth.

Adele said that as soon as I held Rupert she immediately felt him calm. 'It was incredible,' she told me later. What Adele found even more incredible was that simultaneously, Rupert seemed to come alive – his senses heightened. The change in Rupert as I worked with him was instant and dramatic. Adele takes up the story:

'I watched in utter disbelief as Rupert pushed the door of his carrier open, and confidently appeared as though keen to explore the studio set-up. This was a rabbit who was completely agoraphobic, even in his familiar home surroundings, and here he was exploring a strange environment in front of a large group of unfamiliar people! I then picked up a message in my mind from Rupert quite clearly and loudly: "HERE I AM!" I knew that his soul had been awakened, as if the lights had been turned on inside him and he was seeing the world for the first time. It was such a joy for me to see Rupert looking so happy.

'As I came out of the studio I was stopped by one of the presenters who asked me to say a few words that would be edited in after our slot with Margrit. I blurted out: "Amazing! I can't believe the change in Rupert!" I was very tearful, because it seemed that a miracle had just taken place. To witness this change in Rupert was priceless.'

Over the years I have kept in touch with Adele and she regularly updated me on Rupert's progress. After our meeting Rupert improved by hops and leaps. He formed a bond with three other bucks and would charge around with them outside. Rupert had a great quality of life until he passed away aged eleven years. It was wonderful for me to meet this special angel and to play a vital role in his rehabilitation.

Cosmo the marriage counsellor

A cream tabby, with amber-coloured eyes, Cosmo was a stunning-looking cat. He was watching me from a lofty position on top of a kitchen unit as I scribbled some notes on my consultation form. Cosmo's middle-aged owners had acquired him as a kitten and he was now four years old. He had always been a contented puss, never causing them any concern, but in the last few months he had started suffering from nightmares which resulted in him suddenly waking from deep sleep and leaping across the room. Cosmo had been thoroughly checked out by vets and no physical problem had been found, so they were as puzzled as his owners as to why he was acting so bizarrely. Hence I had been called in to see if the cat would divulge the reason for his odd behaviour.

Putting down my pen, I asked a question out loud to Cosmo, to show the owners the sort of thing that I would be saying to him: 'Why is your sleep so disturbed?'

Cosmo did not answer, instead looking beyond me in a typically vague cat way. Obviously I hadn't been clear enough, so I resorted to using his language and repeated the question mind to mind. I had hardly got the question out before sensations of apprehension and sadness washed over me. They were coming from Cosmo.

'They argue a lot,' communicated Cosmo. 'It makes me feel tense and on tenterhooks.'

The cat then settled into a squatting position, his body looking taut. 'She starts the rows,' he continued, and said with emphasis, '*She* is very short-tempered with *him*.' I couldn't help but briefly glance across at the woman, who was sitting next to her husband. They were both watching me quizzically, and it was embarrassing to be discussing them under their noses – I hoped that like their cat, my expression was not giving anything away. I asked Cosmo if it had always been like this, because until recently he had seemed contented. He communicated that the woman had always been prone to moodiness, but nothing like her unpredictable anger nowadays.

The cat had given me a problem – somehow, I had to broach what sounded like a domestic issue. I needed time to think about how I was going to handle this, so I sat quietly staring at Cosmo, who continued to communicate his anxiety. After a few minutes of my verbal silence the man turned to me and asked if Cosmo was saying anything. As tactfully as I could I explained that he was a hypersensitive cat and so would be particularly affected by negative ambience in the home. 'You know, like arguments or raised voices, that sort of thing.'

The man turned to his wife and said to her, 'Well, you are quite snappy these days, my dear,' whereupon she immediately turned to him and shouted loudly: 'No, I am not!!!'

They then sat there glaring at each other and you would have had to have been made of stone not to pick up the chilly and strained atmosphere. I could see exactly what Cosmo meant.

Cosmo jumped down from the cupboard and sat by the door. It was obvious that he wanted to get away from another argument. I had to try to resolve this problem in front of Cosmo, so I continued to talk about the topic of conflicts, explaining how this could adversely affect a pet's temperament, including his or her sleeping habits. It was important to encourage the couple to see that their constant bickering was compromising the wellbeing of their cat, who they both insisted they loved very much. If they wanted to help Cosmo they needed to understand that they should first resolve their tendency to quarrel. We all have spats with our partners but if our bickering becomes incessant then action needs to be taken for everyone's benefit.

I didn't need to know the root cause of their arguments, but I carefully got them to open up about their problem in relation to Cosmo. They talked about Cosmo and the years they had had him. They remembered bringing him home from where he was born, the woman carrying him gently inside her coat and later taking him to bed so that her body warmth would settle him. He had been such a tiny and vulnerable scrap of life. The man recounted the funny things that Cosmo had done, like the time when he had pulled the curtains down onto the head of a cat-hating work colleague who was dropping off some paperwork, and another occasion when he ran across wet cement leaving paw prints which still remained on the path – a happy souvenir of his exuberant youth.

Tearfully, the woman picked Cosmo up and soothed him on her lap, and her husband reached over and joined in the stroking. They both expressed regret that their beloved cat's sense of peace had been influenced by their arguments and resolved to make changes, all of which I communicated to Cosmo.

Our meeting did have a happy outcome. A visit to the doctor revealed that the woman was suffering from an adverse reaction to the medication she was taking for a heart condition and a new prescription helped her to feel much better about life in general. On returning three weeks later, I was delighted to hear that Cosmo had not had a single nightmare, much to the relief of his – now more laid-back – owners. As I was being updated, Cosmo appeared from the garden with a piece of leaf in his mouth.

'Hello Cosmo, nice to see you, how are you? Anything we should discuss?' I asked this counselling cat. Cosmo batted the leaf around before pouncing and rolling on it as it flipped over. Eventually I heard him say, 'It's good now,' and that was it. There was nothing more to be said. Picking up the leaf, Cosmo headed out into the sunshine to do whatever cats do on a fine summer's day.

Smelling stories

Fay and Alan took on two-year-old German shepherd dog Megan, after reading her story on an animal shelter website. It was obvious that Megan came with a lot of baggage. She was very wary of strangers and flinched dramatically every time someone put their hand out or suddenly lifted an arm, tell-tale signs that she had been hit. The dog was nervy and did not settle for long, clinging to Fay and whining if she was out of sight. Four weeks after the couple took Megan on, I got to meet her.

I let Megan investigate my clinic room as I made notes, wanting her to approach me in her own time. There was much to admire about her and I mentioned what I liked to Megan – her pretty sable colouring, beautiful bright eyes and smart new red collar. Megan gave me the cue that she was ready for a more in-depth conversation by touching my hand with her nose, so I got to work. Images emerged in my mind of Megan confined in a small dark space, crushed by sacks. As I passed this information on to Fay, she nodded and said that it made sense. Megan was terrified of the dark and of being in a room with the door closed. Fay also mentioned that she had forgotten to tell me that the reason the man had given for handing her in to the sanctuary, was that she was unruly and uncontrollable. It seemed the man's solution for curbing Megan's boisterous youthful activity was to wedge her in a cupboard, instead of taking her for long satisfying walks.

Having sorted this message out, Megan revealed that she had been tormented for the amusement of visitors. They would put food down and when Megan went to eat, the bowl was taken away and the dog reprimanded with: 'No, you can't have it!' Fay told me that information was really helpful because Megan had been skinny when she arrived in their home, yet they had problems getting her to eat. When food was put down Megan would creep forward and look at Fay as if to say, 'Can I eat it?' Even when Fay encouraged her, Megan would pick at the food and often leave it for the cats to finish off.

Lying on the floor at my feet Megan sighed. 'I sleep now. I never used to rest properly, always alert, waiting for trouble. I can sleep now. And I have started to dream.' Apparently, a couple of days earlier Megan had slept so deeply that at first Fay was worried about her. Then Fay saw her twitching and she knew that Megan was dreaming.

'What do you dream about?' I asked Megan.

'Smelling things ... smelling stories,' she replied.

If I were a dog then that would be a fine dream to have.

And so it was that Megan finally became her true self and was able to realise her potential. Arriving back home, Fay noticed that Megan was less apprehensive, and when they had a houseful of people later that week, it did not faze her at all. Megan was eating better too, as though enjoying food for the first time in her life. And Megan started to play; like a puppy, she would toss around soft toys that had previously been ignored.

'Megan says thank you for releasing her from her bad memories,' Fay wrote in an update email. 'Such a changed dog. Brilliant.'

A rabbit could daydream, a cat had sweet dreams in the sunshine, and a dog's dreams had come true. Angels deserve to be happy.

*

If you have felt moved by the stories in this book then you have animal communication and healing gifts within you. The sort of miracles that I describe can be activated and shared by anyone who wants to expand their knowledge and have a deeper understanding of the human–animal bond.

Pets through their love touch our hearts and our souls, because that's what angels do. Loving a pet means that we become part of the family of angels.

The stories our pets have to tell never end.

My special thanks ...

... start by going to Judith Kendra, Publishing Director of Rider Books, who has her pulse on the zeitgeist. Every time Judith offers me a commission the idea is very timely. My brilliant editor Sue Lascelles expertly guides me and, when I stare into the author's abyss of mental block and approaching deadlines, cajoles me with her good humour and support. Copy editor Helen Pisano also did a great job. My special thanks to Bob Vickers for the design and to the whole team at Rider Press, including PR manager Caroline Newbury.

I am indebted to vets Sue Devereux and Nick Thompson for advice and text checking, and to Nick Thompson, Cheryl Sears and Marcie Fallek for veterinary advice and case studies. Also a big thank you to Dr Anne McBride, course director of the post graduate diploma in companion animal behaviour counselling at Southampton University, for advice about animal behaviour.

My thanks as always go to chartered veterinary physiotherapist and colleague Amanda Sutton for everything that she does to help animals. Thank you too to the Reverend Len Lunn for inspirational chats about spirituality and animals.

I'm grateful to my family and friends for their sacrifices and understanding as I took time out from a social life to complete the book. Huge thank you hugs to my cats Teddy and Lilly for taking up vigil in my office whilst I wrote, encouraging me to take breaks and have fun with them.

Special thanks go to the animals that people bring to me ... and the people that animals introduce me to. I have had so many amazing experiences and look forward to finding out more about their role in our lives.

A heart-felt thank you to pets, horses, birds and wild creatures for your healing soul conversations.